A Way Of Spiritual Experience

ZEN IN JAPANESE ART

ZEN
IN JAPANESE ART

A Way of Spiritual Experience

by

TOSHIMITSU HASUMI

Translated from the German by
JOHN PETRIE

NEW YORK
PHILOSOPHICAL LIBRARY

Published 1962
by Philosophical Library, Inc.
15 East 40th Street, New York 16, N.Y.

Translated from the German
ZEN IN DER JAPANISCHEN KUNST

© *Otto Wilhelm Barth-Verlag 1960*
English translation
© *Routledge & Kegan Paul Ltd 1962*

Printed in Great Britain

CONTENTS

v

PREFACE

ART IS the form-language of the human soul. We men make this form-language our own in joy and in sorrow and no less in the trivial round. Art is not just an external influence upon nature. Our own souls are what we must employ to give a new form and a new meaning to nature or the world. Constant striving after psychic and artistic expression in life—that is the be-all and the way of the art of Japan. The soul lends a new meaning to form; it seeks in artistic expression to disclose the harmony of the cosmic revelation.

The beautiful is the revealing principle of the cosmos. A twinkling star in the sky, a simple flower breathing its fragrance in the meadow, a band of cloud in the blue of heaven—these embody the beautiful as a wondrous manifestation of the cosmos, in which the idea of the Absolute is immanent. That idea gives a hint of the eternal and inconceivable SOMETHING.

The modest flower on the grass verge can create

a special aesthetic atmosphere. A short poem of a few lines can render the true and profound meaning of life. A brush-stroke in water-colour, a few branches in flower arrangement, show us the secret of the beautiful in life. In the pure soul the world manifests the profundity of the beautiful. The more profound the soul, the greater its purity. Art is the giving of form to the formless. This giving of form is fully complementary (in the sense of being incomplete without that which it is itself required to complete). Thus the formless ground becomes visible behind the formed, but only in glimpses. The way of art helps us to penetrate deep into the inner structure of the cosmos. A form, a colour or a composition embody the absolute meaning of the cosmos: a composition is world-creation in artistic forms.

This psychic way the Japanese calls 'Zen'. In Zen the relation between Absolute and cosmos receives its form from man. Man is the revelation of the Absolute in the cosmos: he is a mirror of the All. The forms are an unmediated expression of the cosmic experience of man.

In Zen the basic law of the cosmos manifests itself. This is the path to the ULTIMATE, the HIGHEST and the DEEPEST—or, as the Japanese conceive it, the NOTHING—in other words, GOD as inwardly revealed. The reciprocal relation between NOTHING and revelation is maintained by means of the perception of being and the experience of life. Yet the whole—the cosmos itself—is at the same time only the shadow of the NOTHING, of being and of appearance. That is why Japanese art selects various qualities, all based on principle.

The characteristic quality of Japanese art is its intimate connection with the immanent world. Love of nature not only shows the way to contemplative transcendence: even more it is a guide into the meditative world of the spirit. Art reveals itself in psychic understanding of the inner essence of things, and gives form to the relation of man with the Nothing, with the nature of the Absolute. It sees the features of the Absolute in ordinary life and gives them expression, direct, unmediated and formative.

In the autumn wind man feels the eternal transience of things: in the soundless fall of leaves he senses that his existence is given to him once and once only. In this experience of the moment Japanese feeling instantly transcends itself and enters those depths of the cosmic world which are the shadows of the NOTHING, and in which the existence of the individual is anchored.

The second quality of Japanese art is its effort to attain simplicity. If the Absolute is to be directly grasped, the many-coloured world must be seen through, and everything inessential must be eliminated. This psychic process of effort we call 'Zen'. Zen is that principle of psychic unity which forms itself in simplicity and yet is manifest in contrariety. This psychic unity appears in the way people think, in their every spiritual activity; and it is often evinced by the fragmentary in form and the paradoxical in content. The simpler the soul, the more complementary, that is, incomplete in itself, is its expression.

The third psychic peculiarity is intuition. Intuitive creation is the characteristic feature of Japanese art, which in this is quite the opposite of Western art with its strongly rational cast. Intuition is the faculty of comprehending the object of the soul in its interior relation with the cosmic totality lying concealed under the variety of the world. The task of intuition is to orient the inwardness of the human soul towards the NOTHING.

The fourth quality is the relation of the Japanese to the intentional formation of ideas. This peculiarity comes out quite clearly, particularly in the conception of God. The Japanese conceives the Absolute, not as the persona, the self-determination, of the Absolute, but as the NOTHING, as undetermined Something, as essence, which is the nature of the

Absolute. The way to the NOTHING is the inner-most art of Japan, and out of it all formative art un-folds.

These four qualities can be recognized throughout the range of Japanese art. But all art is so fashioned as to be in its qualities an inward reflection of the principles of the cosmos. In the endless variety of the world of nature we glimpse a unitary inner order, and the unitary outward form must give expression to variety.

The most important aesthetic principle is harmony—harmony of forms, colours, and materials, harmony of expression, harmony of order, harmony of place and time; harmony of heaven, earth, and man; harmony of harmonies.

All Japanese art calls for complete mastery of technique, developed by reflection within the soul of man. Outward technique by itself is not art. It is only through long training of the soul that the pupil is brought to the true inward technique. In art it is not merely a question of artistic dexterity, but of the artistic process within the artist. It is the 'art-less art', and its meaning is 'art of the soul'. For us Japanese the arrangement of colours, composition and line-forms means a step on the way to the absolute aesthetic world of the soul. That is 'Zen in art'.

Japanese art is neither more nor less than an art of

the soul: in it inward and outward art flow together.

Rigorous technical and psychic exercises show the way into the secret of cosmic life. In the Zen of Japanese art the typical Japanese peculiarity of psychic experience becomes manifest. Everything that is formed in art is united with the human soul. The working of the soul penetrates the practical life of every day. Creation in art is the psychic unfolding of the personality, which is rooted in the NOTH-ING—in other words, in GOD. Its effect is a deepening of the personal dimension of the soul. By taking the way of 'Zen in art' we experience the basic ground of the cosmos, in which all existence is enclosed.

Artistic skill, therefore, does not mean artistic perfection: it remains rather a continuing medium or reflection of some step in psychic development, the perfection of which is not to be found in form and shape, but must radiate from the human soul.

The artistic activity of the Japanese does not consist in art itself as such: it penetrates into a deeper world in which all art-forms of things inwardly experienced flow together, and in which the harmony of soul and cosmos in the NOTHING has its outcome in reality.

Fribourg   T. HASUMI
September 1959

The nature of art is the art of nature.

I

INTRODUCTION

OUR INQUIRY concerning the essence of art—and the answer is not easily found —must take second place to an inquiry into the essence of culture. It is relevant in this context that all culture is founded on the independence and capacity for self-determination of the human soul as contrasted with the rest of the world of nature.[1] Culture does not consist simply of nature and primitive human activity, but is a system constructed by the free soul, built up on the basis of nature by means of personal actions and laying claim to universal understanding. It is particularly in art that the aesthetic aspect of culture is reflected, for art is that function of culture in which the aesthetic mirroring of the world is broken up in its passage through a personal I, and at the same time finds its interpretation. The task of art is so to state in aesthetic creation the deepest psychic and personal experiences of a human being as to enable those experiences to be intelligible and generally recognized within the total framework of an ideal world.

Art is on the one hand the expression of a personal experience, on the other of the universally human; each component complements the other. This peculiar dual character of art makes it more difficult for the person considering a work of art to understand foreign cultures; for everyone is at home in his own cultural atmosphere and finds the aesthetic expression of the universally human most readily in the culture of his own country.

There are in the world very few cultures which in the course of their history have acquired, through long psychic experience, the power to set the inexpressible and deepest ground—the Nothing—at the central point of their artistic formation. The historical condition on which alone this high psychic experience becomes possible requires above all a continuous and profound tradition of transcendence, just as in general tradition is one of the most important factors in the formation of what at any given time constitutes historical reality.[2] Tradition is the uninterrupted and formative objectivization of continuing and progressive creative strength. Culture is in general the synthesis resulting from the encounter between the tradition handed down and the personal development of the individual entity. Without tradition there would be no basis for the rise of national cultures.

More than that, personal character, which can be developed only on the basis of cultural tradition, is itself in turn midway between the particular cultural character of one's own people and the universally human which transcends it. It is worth noting that the very endeavour to understand a foreign culture develops the comprehensiveness and liveliness of the capacity for understanding one's own tradition.

It may be asserted that the works of art of Europe and Japan are in many respects similar, and such similarities may, in fact, be found: but such a method of proceeding is quite alien to the right way of looking at art, because it must always remain one-sided and purely external. A work of art can only be rightly understood as a whole in the setting of a total culture. For this reason a theory of art which aims at a clear definition of a foreign culture must always and necessarily derive from an understanding of the total cultural setting. Most particularly, it must convey the real spiritual background and the underlying metaphysical traditions, for it is on these that art lives and thrives. This way of proceeding is necessary in considering Japanese art

3

because it has its origin in a closed insular society; and the Japanese, as islanders, have developed a quite different outlook on the world, a different way of thinking and a different feeling for life. In Japanese art the peculiar character of the Japanese people can be caught at its purest. Before the sixteenth century Japanese life was still entirely untouched by European influences. It is from this enclosed situation that all the characteristic peculiarities of Japanese art-forms and types grew up, and have for the most part maintained themselves and followed their own line of development up to the present day.

Japanese art is to be understood not only as aesthetic art, if we may so put it, but also as a comprehensive attitude to life embracing the entire life of soul and spirit. In Japan this is designated as 'artless art', by which is meant the art of the soul which far transcends mere artistic skill. Japanese art includes not only the formative arts in the European sense, such as literature, painting, sculpture, architecture, and lacquer work—in Japan flower arrangement, the tea ceremony, swordsmanship, archery, Judo etc., also come into this category. It also covers the formless art of the interior life, at which all the other arts are aiming. Art in the Japanese sense is the endeavour to carry over into ordinary

4

existence the infinitely deep, inexpressible, and unknowable ground of living: it is in Japan the way to the Absolute. For this reason everything is included that pertains to the moral way of life of humanity, and quite essentially to art—a conception of life which, in this mode of thinking, Europe scarcely knows.

II

THE JAPANESE OUTLOOK
ON THE WORLD AS THE SPIRITUAL
BACKGROUND TO
JAPANESE CULTURE [3]

A PEOPLE'S outlook on the world is the expression of its profoundest spiritual essence. That is the source from which it acquires that perceptible form of typical character specially to be found among the Japanese people, whose outlook on life is based on a threefold spiritual foundation. Their oldest spiritual possession stems from the ancestor cult of mythical Japan, to be found in Shinto, which testifies to the profound reverence of the Japanese people for their past. Secondly, the political life and feeling of the Japanese, together with their social, political, and moral standards, bear the strong impress of Confucianism and are directed to the present.

The third spiritual force is Buddhism. This,

coming from India by way of China, brought its influence to bear in particular by forming and developing a religious mindfulness of the future and the passion which the Japanese has for eternity.

Of all the elements that go to form the Japanese outlook on the world, Shinto is the most characteristic and primitive expression of the Japanese national soul. This mythos of the earliest times is so strongly and deeply rooted in the history and soul of the Japanese people that even under the later shaping of the reflecting mind this primitive element has maintained itself for thousands of years with constant and continuing immediacy, and has endured into the most recent past like an ancient and venerable rock. Shinto is not a religion in the European sense, but an ancestor cult, a primitive folk sentiment, which, as a cult, dominates the entire national life of Japan, and underlies the innate and ultimately inexpressible rhythm of the folk-life of the Japanese. That which in its capacity of state cult and mythos has acquired visible form, dwells deep and formless in the heart of every individual Japanese.

In contrast to this emotional characteristic of the Japanese consciousness of life stands a principle of highly restrictive moulding of life—Confucianism with all its austerity and stiffly formal ethical and moral philosophy. Confucianism derives from the primitive moral and ethical rules of Chinese society, which it clamped into a closed system, giving it thereby a spiritual order. The acceptance by the Japanese of Confucianism is no ground for being misled into thinking that the original feeling for life of the Chinese people is anything but totally different from that of the Japanese. It would be erroneous to infer on this account that the two peoples are inwardly akin. The only reason why the Japanese took over the social doctrines established by Confucianism was that these doctrines furnished them in the earliest times with the fundamental ideas for an ordered social life. What Confucianism primarily developed in ancient Japan was the strong feeling for order throughout political and moral activity, and this led to the creation of a firm structure of social life founded on moral laws. Even today, despite all modern deviations, Confucianism is a part of the Japanese soul. This firm original basic structure, preconscious and non-rational, of moral standards and regulations is still twined round with a flourishing growth of practical rules for living, customs, usages, and strict etiquette.

The third spiritual basic force, still at work in Japan to the present day, is Buddhism. The general spiritual trend in Japan is inseparable from the

Buddhist atmosphere and tradition; for, over a period of some 1,400 years, Buddhism, in several varieties of the Mahayana version, has exercised its powerful influence on the soul of the Japanese and has been the source of a profound spiritual life. Mahayana Buddhism can be characterized as pantheistic. It is permeated by the basic idea that Buddha is in all things, and that all things possess Buddha, that is, nature. All things, all beings, are predestined to Buddhahood and so to absorption in Buddha. According to the Buddhist conception there is no essential difference between Buddhahood and nature. Both in principle are the same in their being. Buddha is the essence of nature as existent. Nature is a mode of being of the Nothing, the spirit. The man who has attained the highest realization has become Buddha. He returns to nature and so into a mode of being of the Nothing. The ultimate and all-embracing, in whose domain all that exists is determination and has being, in which our thinking, feeling, perceiving self finds its deepest ground, in which all opposites are blotted out in reality, the ultimate expression of all that exists, in which realization awakes and loses itself again—that highest and ultimate is the Nothing.[4] The Nothing is transcendent and immanent unity, in which the opposites and tensions are abolished, and the soul knows in its profoundest depths that it was born in the world as a pure mirror of primal consciousness.[5]

By soul we understand the Nothing which is confined to and determined by the self and which consists in this very confinement and determination, whereas in God as the absolute Nothing opposites are no longer possible.

In order to be able to grasp the essence of the world present in every existent, there is a need for a mode of contemplation that disregards the specificity of all things and comes to the experience of the transcendent-immanent, to the experience, that is, of all-oneness, which is the universal link binding the world together. With the disappearance of the specificity of things, and also of the specificity of the human self, man is absorbed by the absolute oneness in the absolute void, in the 'Nothing'. Absorption into the absolute void, into the Nothing, brings about the experience of the oneness of every existent, absolute rest, absolute freedom and deliverance from all sorrows. The soul is plunged into and overwhelmed in the eternal sea of the Nothing—which is also that ground from which it springs up again.

From what was said earlier concerning the unity and holiness of nature in the Shinto feeling for life, it is easy to understand how Mahayana Buddhism was able to strike deep roots in Japan and to fashion an inner unity of life hand in hand with the native Shintoism. Although Mahayana Buddhism is not characterized as pessimistically hostile to life, but has a positive significance—as opposed to the original Indian form of Hinayana Buddhism—this is nevertheless not to be understood as implying personality in the pantheistic sense to which attention has been drawn. The basic metaphysical concept of the Nothing acquires positive significance by virtue of the doctrine of the identity of absolute denial and absolute affirmation, of the one and the many, of immanence and transcendence. He who has been enlightened realizes the deepest spiritual dimension of the Nothing. The abandonment of the negative and pessimistic attitude fundamental to Indian Hinayana Buddhism worked itself out slowly in Tibet and China, and was completed in Japan. This development extends from the middle ages, particularly from the time of Dogen (1200–1253),[6] to the modern Japan of the twentieth century, where the Japanese philosophers Nishida[7] and Tanabe[8] have taken hold of Mahayana Buddhism and systematically developed it as a metaphysic.

Of all the sects widespread in Japan, Shingon, Judo and Zen Buddhism are the most important. Shingon is a school of Buddhism which preaches a pantheistic personalism. According to it, the supreme divine rank is that taken by Dainichi Buddha, of whom everything else that exists is no more than an appearance. Dainichi is the 'word' of the cosmos, and this 'word' is a holy symbol of every existence in the world. Out of Tendai mysticism, which has a close inner kinship with Shingon mysticism, there developed the Judo school, which believes in the absolute grace of Amidha Buddha. Its adherents pray to Amidha Buddha that they may be absorbed in the eternal ocean of grace.

Zen is the most important religion in Japan, and the one with the profoundest metaphysical basis, which does not believe in the power of grace. It is hardly possible now to realize how much the development and deepening of Japanese culture in its entirety, but particularly in philosophy and art, is indebted to Zen Buddhism.

The essence of Zen is not something the European can grasp offhand. Zen is not a philosophy in the European sense. Buddhist schools such as, for example, Shingon, Tendai, and Kegon are much richer in logical and metaphysical speculation. Zen is not a theology. In contrast to the theological bases of religion, Zen is the living practice of man striving for deliverance. Zen is not rational, nor yet related to mysticism—despite its origin in

Indian yoga [9]—for the mystical experience is based on ecstasy.

Zen is not a theology or a philosophy, and it possesses no dogma. It is the immediate, and therefore inexpressible, individual experience whose aim is inner enlightenment. Enlightenment itself occurs suddenly, like a lightning flash: it is the 'satori' of the Japanese. The 'satori' experience is an inward event that occurs only once, but persists throughout life. This experience grows into a capacity that can be realized at any time. It depends essentially on a contradiction that cannot be grasped by formal thought. For something would have to be expressed which is simply inexpressible. Undoubtedly the artistic formation and way of thinking of the Japanese, based as it is on the wholeness and self-contained nature of human existence, is deeply indebted to the influence of Zen. In so far as we still encounter contradiction and a dialectic form of logic in Japanese philosophy (particularly that of Nishida and Tanabe) we have to do with an inner experience flowing from that of Zen.[10]

Zen is also not an ethic, and knows nothing of the question 'What ought I to do?' It does not teach the value of an individual action, but the man of Zen knows without reflection how he ought to act. He has entire freedom in all his doing.

13

Nevertheless we still do not know what Zen really is, just because Zen cannot be grasped with words. In order to experience this, we must enter a Zen monastery and take part in the zazen (Zen meditation exercises) under the guidance of a profound and experienced master. We must learn through control of breathing to attain unity of soul and body, and at the same time to feel incessant shocks within. Then the soul mirrors itself suddenly in itself, and a hidden inward tide of strength overflows. When after decades of striving and exercise we attain enlightenment, we still cannot say what Zen really is, because the essential remains inexpressible. Only the experienced Zen master is capable of recognizing and understanding the man who has been transformed by enlightenment. Human understanding is not based on a rational foundation, but consists largely in a spiritual approach, that is, in reciprocal communication.

Zen is all-embracing knowledge. Analytic perception is an obstacle to the true Zen-experience. Perception is only the beginning, and a part, of all experience. The man who attains the dimension of contradictory expression must recognize where the limit of reason is drawn. The man who transcends the scale of reason—who reaches the point where the intellect falls silent—enters the realm in which the soul operates fully and freely and makes contact with the Nothing.

By means of enlightenment the whole world, too, is bathed in a new and different light and everything takes on a different, deeper meaning. Man himself has become, from within outwards, calm, strong, and serene. A stone, a plant, the song of a bird, even a shred of flying cloud, points to the ultimate, all-embracing Something. Man's every faculty of soul and body rings with a new note, and is felt as richer than ever before in blessing, peace, and joy.[11]

According to what can be concluded from the unmediated but contradictory statements concerning 'satori'—a prelogical intuition—enlightenment is concerned particularly with uncovering the essence of the world in its own self. It is the way of direct experience, of the profoundest human experience, of seeing into the essence of one's own self. It is only through zazen meditation that such a profound insight is gained, only thus that the soul is enabled to enter the realm which enlightens and is enlightened. It is at once a cleansing, a freeing and an emptying of the soul. To the man enlightened by 'satori' the soul has become transparent in a flash. The ground of being shines forth from everything that exists.

If we are to believe all that has been written

about Zen, the important thing is that man in his own existence manifests being itself.[12] In these conditions the human soul finds itself able to pass through every spiritual adventure. When the ultimate Nothing is attained, the oppositions of every day are transcended. Yet this experience can still be expressed only by means of the contradiction inevitably inherent in every statement about Zen. Moreover, the primal opposition between the I and the world, between consciousness and its object, has disappeared. That is to say, experience has grown into primal consciousness, the Nothing has been attained. The ultimate experience of all-oneness in the Nothing gives rise to that calmness of existence so peculiar to Zen. We see the pure form of the world as it was in the beginning. In the context of such an experience painters employ sparing but sure brush-strokes to create a picture of the landscape full of profound meaning, in which the very stones come alive on the canvas. Poets likewise, sparing in the use of words, depict some piece of nature in which the meaning of eternity can be felt. The Nothing is in everything.

The fundamental characteristic of Zen is a life of enlightenment. All the moments of our existence in this temporal life constitute a flow of decisions and have the capacity to develop into the self-revelation of being.[13] It is not to be wondered at that the Japanese finds it easy to understand Heidegger's philosophy of the progressive manifestation of being in human existence by way of the Nothing, or Jasper's philosophy of the illumination of existence on the horizon of the transcendent—though, to the Japanese mind, both are far from satisfying.

Zen is not simply restricted to Buddhism. It is something to be experienced in every field of man's spiritual activity. We can follow Zen and at the same time be Buddhist or Christian, scientist or plain manual labourer. All that Zen does is to awaken the primal consciousness hidden within us which alone makes possible any spiritual activity.

To sum up—Zen is strength, concentrated, universal, utterly free, attained by complete emptying of the consciousness; it is life, inwardly enlightened and fulfilled; it is absolute inner freedom, perfectly dispensed at every instant. We constantly meet it, constantly breathe its air, in the absolute Nothing.

In the Nothing all things remain things, nature remains nature, being remains being, contradiction remains contradiction. In the Nothing the All takes its bearings on the All. The Nothing is the mirror of of all that has being.

III

THE METAPHILOSOPHY OF ART [14]

SEEN FROM this point of view, the beautiful
is that which in transcendent fashion gives
form in space and time to the Nothing. At the
same time art is an unending immanent development of the soul, a revelation, within limits, of the
Nothing in the individual being. The idea of the
beautiful is a personal and particular insight into
the essence of the soul in a form appropriate to
transcendent-immanent reality. Where the harmony between outer and inner is achieved in
aesthetic form, where the artist endows the cosmos
and his own self with expression—there the immanent, subjective activity of the personality
achieves the height of transcendent objectivity.[15]
Subjectivity can realize itself only in so far as it
gives itself shape by entering into the objective
world. Subjective immanence and objective transcendence are inextricably linked in creative art.
Only when the painter stands brush in hand in

18

front of the canvas does the way to a unique eternal idea open before him.[16] When a poet enters at one glance into the heart of nature, the idea translates itself into speech in the same instant. Creative art has a profound operation on the soul.

The more deeply grounded the artist's soul, the more original it is[17]. In its originality the world manifests the depths of the beautiful. Together with the concrete personality there is manifested both that which stands behind it and what, as it were, springs from it. The beautiful is the embodiment of the Absolute, mediated through the personality. The ultimate and all-embracing can be apprehended as the metaphysical background of a work. As an expression of the creative spirit, a work of art also mediates that which cannot be directly expressed without mediation.

Because of the hidden character of the background, logical perception is out of the question. The problem is how penetration into the Nothing is to be made accessible to the senses. Extremely difficult though the task is—expressing the inexpressible and giving form to the formless—that is nevertheless how the message conveyed only in hints becomes feasible and intelligible.[18]

The work of art is, so to speak, a portion inseparably connected with the whole, which is itself

19

an essential part of the work. This aesthetic back
ground—the unity embracing everything—can b
clearly understood from the Buddhist art of th
east. The various forms of art are the product of th
connection between the background and what i
brought to realization on it. The general lack o
individuality in Oriental art must derive from th
fact that an essential part of it is this all-embracin
background.[19] The beholder must participate in th
creative process if he is to understand the artisti
background and to share and follow the experienc
it offers. Looking at art is itself an artistic activity
Beginning with the work of art, the beholde
moves on to encounter the all, or the Nothing.

In order to define the indefinable, to express th
inexpressible and to give form to the formless
there is a need for certain ideas borrowed from
connoisseurship which are generally current ir
Japan. By way of indicating the variety of the inner
breadths and depths, the Japanese often uses the
complementary method: he speaks of high breadth,
deep breadth, and flat breadth. At this point the
world of actual reality disappears. Similarly a
distinction is drawn between the spiritual ground,
that which is endowed with form and that which
lacks form. The formless, however, according to the
complementary method, possesses height without

height, depth without depth, breadth without breadth. The world of common sense undergoes a change, and the world of transcendent intuition alone remains.

When we make our way through the formed and the formless, and pursue a sympathetic vibration and consonance deep into the unfathomable ground of our soul, the effect is that the ground of our own self and the ground of the world are the one all-embracing Nothing. In the Nothing there is neither inner nor outer, neither above nor below. The Nothing comes thence from where the Nothing is and thither the Nothing goes. In it is heard a faint sound echoing in the human soul.

A life based on this formless ground of the Nothing is not pessimistic in the European sense. On the contrary, it includes, as we have seen, personality, creative act and deliverance; it is a life utterly fulfilled. It is precisely in this fulfilled life that we find a characteristic feature of the Oriental outlook on the world.[20] If we go further in this direction, we come, in accordance with the complementary method, into contact with an art of sadness without the shadow of sadness, an art of joy without the colour of joy—as can be recognized in the pictures of Sesshu. It is the art of the soul at peace, through which—like moonlight mirrored in a deep lake—

the light of eternity pours calmly down on the ground of the soul. Moon and lake, soul and heaven, earth and man fashion art for ever.

The deep comprehension acquired by contact with the Nothing runs like an echo or a following wave through every condition of human existence: it is truth itself. In this context Shinto is, as it were, the folk-rhythm of Japanese life in state, province, district, and family, whereas Buddhism fashions a special content, and addresses itself solely to the individual and his metaphysical situation.[21] True, Japanese history tells how, shortly after the acceptance of Buddhism, there were struggles for power between Shintoism, Confucianism, and Buddhism: but today complete harmony has been attained, as is apparent in the way of life of the Japanese people. All Japanese are more or less Shintoist and Buddhist at the same time.

This inner transformation seems to be the source that gave rise to the school of thought which, in the shape of Zen, set Buddhism free from every specific form, and developed into the soul-rhythm of life—not (in contrast to Shintoism) of the national cult, but of the individual religious life.[22]

In Japanese philosophy the Nothing, with its historical origin in Zen Buddhism, is the exact opposite of a world-denying, pessimistic nihilism.

LIFE-AFFIRMING

The Metaphilosophy of Art

On the basis of such a world-denying nihilism, art would properly speaking be meaningless. Zen is not nihilism or pessimism: least of all is it positivism. Japanese Zen Buddhism claims to be absolutely life-affirming. It is in this sense that Japanese philosophy, with its conception of being as the self-unfolding of the unformed Nothing, finds its deepest foundation in the Japanese outlook on the world.

The many-sidedness of the Japanese outlook, arising and changing on the foundation of Shintoism, Confucianism, and Buddhism, is accompanied by a common characteristic: practical and theoretical factors are outweighed by the emotional. This last maintains itself in the totality of human existence, and forcibly rejects one-sided rationalism and intellectualism, because the rationalist point of view makes it quite impossible for the structural totality of man and the world ever to be apprehended or experienced. At once philosopher, poet, painter, master of swordsmanship and the tea ceremony, of archery and flower arrangement— thus it is that the ultimate aim of the Japanese is to use his daily activity to become a pastmaster of life, and so to lay hold of the art of living. Philosophers, men of learning, and masters in all branches of art must first be masters in living, for the soul creates everything. The whole of human life is a liturgy on

the Nothing. In the end every man must bow before the Absolute:

> I know not what
> Is here enshrined.
> Only the tears
> Well up from my heart
> Overflowing with reverence
>
> PRIEST SAIGYO (1121–1193)

The most important problem, however, lies in
the fact that Europe and the Far East look out on the
world in quite opposite fashion. It may perhaps be
thought that Zen is a non-Christian 'religion'. But
hardly anywhere else than in Zen is so deep a
human experience of primal consciousness to be
found. Christianity is a manifestation of the incarnation of God, whereas Zen is an intensive, inward
enlightening of the divine being, which the Japanese
has apprehended as Nothing, and which must be
supplemented, uplifted, and completed by means of
manifestation in the incarnation of God, so that both
components must approach, touch, and pass over
into one another.

IV

AN HISTORICAL SURVEY OF THE ARTISTIC AND SPIRITUAL HISTORY OF JAPAN [23]

IT IS very difficult to mark off one period in the history of art precisely from another, and, particularly in the context of a history of culture, clear delimitation is impossible. History is the living biography of mankind, and the task of history as a science is to explain the links in the development of human existential experience. It ought, however, to be possible to establish fairly specific historical characters and types of art. From the sequence of these basic characters and types spring the different historical periods. These, in the case of Japan, can be set out in seven epochs:

1. The period before the influence of Buddhism (up to A.D. 549).

2. The first Buddhist cultural period—Japanese early Middle Ages (up to A.D. 794).

3. The period of the growth of a purely Japanese culture—Japanese central Middle Ages, the 'Hei-an'

25

period, as it is called, lasting to the end of the twelfth century.

4. The second Buddhist cultural period—Japanese late Middle ages, the 'Kamakura' period as it is called (up to A.D. 1334).

5. The period of the growth of a second purely Japanese culture, the 'Muromachi' period as it is called (up to A.D. 1573). In 1539 the first Europeans came to Japan.

6. The new Japanese cultural period, the 'Tokugawa' or 'Edo' period as it is called (up to A.D. 1868).

7. The modern Japanese cultural period (up to the present day).

According to the imperial historical document *Nippon Shoki* (eighth century A.D.), Japanese history begins in the year 660 B.C. According to *Nippon Shoki*, the first Emperor, Jimmu, founded the empire of Japan in Kashiwara in the province of 'Yamato' in that year. But this date is not really significant for the history of culture. Japanese culture was already well developed before that. Indeed, the importance of the ancient autochthonous art of Japan should not be underrated, for its epoch prepared the way for the extremely rapid development of the succeeding periods. In this sense I conceive of the art of antiquity as an historical precondition for the immediately following period.

26

Two factors constitute the basic conditions for the shaping of a culture—country and people. The islands of Japan lie to the far east of Asia and to the far west of the Pacific Ocean. Climate has a great influence on the shaping and development of a culture. Geographically Japan comprises a number of small island groups, with several variations of climate. In these geographical conditions not a few races and peoples met and mingled. That is why there is no Japanese race properly so called, but only a Japanese people; and it was this people that fashioned a uniform spiritual history and culture. Even before this amalgamation, Japan lay in the sphere of influence of several world-cultures of prehistory. From the north came the outliers, presumably Indo-Germanic, of the Caucasian cultural area. From the south, Japan was penetrated by representatives of the coastal cultural area of India and South-East Asia, and from the west by representatives of the Chinese cultural area coming by way of Korea. This unique mixture of races, with their mentalities and varied cultures, was possible by reason of Japan's isolated situation, and eventually resulted in an entirely new race and culture.

According to the celebrated book by Muraoka, *Introduction to the History of Japanese Culture*, Tokyo, 1938—the original is written in Japanese [24]—early

Chinese traditions have it that the Japanese culture of that first period was already fairly highly developed and accordingly constituted the foundation for the adoption of the higher Chinese culture. Proof of this is to be found in the productions of the dolmen art of the time, particularly in the 'Haniwa' statues, whose artistic value is recognizable despite their naïve character. Many ancient illegible inscriptions on stone are now being excavated throughout Japan.

As early as the year 860 after the foundation of the Japanese empire by the first Emperor Jimmu (A.D. 200), Chinese Confucianism had made its way into Japan and had exercised a great influence on Japanese history and culture. Confucianism is an ethical and political doctrine, not a religion: it contains practically no other-worldly ideas or purely metaphysical speculations. In the sixth century Japan came for the first time into contact with the Buddhist religion. This event was of the utmost importance for the entire development that was to follow. At that time the only spiritual current was Shintoism, also not a religion, but the primal feeling of the Japanese and the basis of their world-outlook. Confucianism strengthened Shintoism and gave it support in the spiritual and political fields: Buddhism gave it its metaphysical foundations. The differences between Shintoism, Confucianism, and Buddhism gave rise to cultural and religious struggles. These did not, however, co-exist in timeless sequence: rather, something new arose instead out of their reciprocal action. The opposition between Japanese and foreign ways of existence did not mean the defeat of the one and the victory of the other, but constituted a permanent enrichment of the psychic and spiritual life of the people. Disintegration would have occurred only if the Japanese element had been overwhelmed and swept away by the foreign. The Japanese people did not consider the foreign element as a sworn enemy, neither did they regard their own as absolute. Consequently these two or three forces, mutually so contradictory, by no means meant a stunting, but an enhancement, of the life of the people. It was from the primal strength of Shintoism that soul and spirit developed, and creative power sprang up as a driving force of progress in the history of Japan. Behind the cult of emperor and ancestors lived and breathed a profound piety, and there is still to be found the light of a belief in creation which—to keep to the Shinto way of speaking—'shines in the soul of the people as well as in the natural landscape'.

Confucianism, however, could do nothing to

bring out the artistic genius latent in the Japanese people. Art is first of all a material expression and objectivization of the profound and basic consciousness and experience of mankind. Confucianism did not concern itself with these things, and so was unable to offer the values of the other world—the very foundation of art. In this sense it could contribute nothing to the development of art and genius.

Buddhism, on the other hand, opened up for Japanese art a variety of hitherto unknown fields. These were accepted by the Japanese of antiquity with wonder and enthusiasm.

The essential importance of this period from the point of view of cultural history lies in the early romantic movement.[25] After the establishment of a closed constitutional state in the fifth and sixth centuries, and the supreme flowering of culture in China, Japanese history was set in the atmosphere of a new spiritual trend. The introduction of Buddhism gave the impulse for the unfolding of Japanese art under Prince Shotuku (A.D. 572–621), a man of deep and genuine piety, its guardian and first great patron. Several of his writings are still accounted masterpieces of Buddhist theology. The Horyu Ji near Nara and the Shitenno Ji in Osaka, which were his first palaces, and were later turned into temples and monasteries, are considered to be the most representative and important pieces of architecture of the period. Horyu Ji is the oldest wooden building in good preservation in the world. The images of the Buddha and the decorative objects installed in the monastery and temple were made with State support. The path of Japanese art was thus opened up by Buddhism. The works of art of this period have almost exclusively Buddhist themes, just as the themes of early mediaeval art in the West are entirely Christian. Other outstanding works of art are the expression of this first Buddhist artistic epoch, known as the 'Suiko' period (seventh century A.D.). Particularly developed were sculpture and architecture. Immediately thereafter followed, by way of further flowerings of the Japanese Buddhist epoch, the 'Hakuho' period and the 'Nara' period, both of them born of the great and stirring strength of the time and constituting the first syntheses between Buddhism and the ancient spirit of Japan.

Hitherto Chinese civilization had been introduced into Japan by way of the Korean peninsula, but at this point Ono no Imoko was sent to China as the first Japanese ambassador to the Court of the Sui dynasty in the fifteenth year of the reign of the Empress Suiko (A.D. 607)—the acting Emperor was

Prince Shotuku. Japan now imported articles of Chinese culture from all parts of the country. This brought with it a great renewal of political, as of cultural, life. In A.D. 604 Prince Shotuku had published the first constitution, which from the outset proceeds on religious and moral principles. He was the first collector of historical documents, though these were unfortunately later lost. At the beginning of the Hakuho period the Taika reforms brought about a great revolution (A.D. 645). In politics this did away with the old class system, and it implemented the centralization of the whole of social life—religion, law, festivals, ranks, costume, holidays, and so on.

Outstanding works of Hakuho art are to be found in architecture, sculpture, and wall-painting. These are still considered as classics of Japanese art. The murals in the Kon-do Hall of the Horyu Ji Temple (built in A.D. 607) are the earliest oil-paintings in the world and constitute one of the supreme achievements of Asiatic art. The tendency of the representative art of the period is realistic. Out of this realism developed the ensuing period, the Nara period.

In the Nara period Japanese art attained its peak. The Empress Gemmyo moved the capital to Nara in 710, and there built the huge Imperial capital city.

In every province a monastery was founded for monks, and also one for nuns. In the time of Shomu, the forty-fifth Emperor (A.D. 701–756), the enthusiasm for Buddhism, which had grown almost into a State religion, increased still further. At Nara, the Imperial capital of the time, the Emperor Shomu built the enormous 'Todaiji' monastery in A.D. 743: this is to this day the biggest wooden building in the world (some 150 feet in height). In the single room of the main building sits a meditating Buddha of copper and gold some 60 feet high. The Emperor Shomu's motive in erecting this monumental building and the enormous Buddha image was not only pious conviction, but also the desire to display his Imperial authority and his wealth to his own people and to make a demonstration against China.

Another monument of his power and great wealth has been preserved for us—his treasury called 'Shoso-In'. Here he collected over three thousand *objets d'art* from the then known world, not only from Japan, but also from China, India, Persia, and even Greece. This collection is still preserved in its ancient form as Imperial property, and offers a survey of the entire culture of the world as it then was.

The special characteristic of the period consists in

the tenderness and perfection of the artistic forms, which are sharply differentiated from the abstract beauty of Indian art and from the oppressive monumentality of the T'ang era in China (618–907). It is the supreme expression of Asiatic art of its period, which manifested its peculiar character in architecture and sculpture, whereas painting was of only secondary importance.

Besides Buddhism and Buddhist art, the culture of the period also included literature and law-giving. A part of the law then codified remained in force until the Meiji restoration in 1868. It is particularly noteworthy that at this time two Imperial historical publications appeared. One is entitled *Kojiki* (A.D. 711)—this was the first mythology—the other, called *Nippon Shoki* (A.D. 710), was the first official Imperial written history. Also important is a collection of poems which likewise was published with Imperial support, the *Mannyo Shu* (A.D. 771) or *Collection of Ten Thousand Leaves*. This collection comprises 4,000 poems, long and short, written by men of all ranks from Emperor to peasant and in all ages from antiquity to its own day. The most important poets are Kakinomoto no Hitomaro (662–710), Otome no Yakamochi (died 785), and Yamabe no Akahito (*circa* 725). The tone of the *Mannyo* poems is strong, free, and virile: yet the

34

style is of a rhetorical character, having a highly refined beauty.

First let us quote an ancient ode by Kakinomoto no Hitomaro, which almost recalls a Hebrew psalm:

> Hills and sea waves
> Surround me:
> Towering up to the sky
> Are the mountains.
> Like foam
> On the surging, thundering waves,
> Man is a nothing
> Born but to die.

Now let us take another poem by Kakinomoto no Hitomaro:

> In the province of Iwami
> Between trees on Takatsunu mountain
> I wonder whether my wife will have seen
> My beckoning hand.

Yamabe no Akahito writes:

> I, who came to the meadow
> To pick violets,
> Slept one whole night
> Feeling how lovely it was there.

35

Another poem by Akahito runs:

> To the bay of Tago
> I come and see
> White-blanketed
> Fuji mountain soar up.
> It is as though the snow were falling on it.

Yamanone no Okura (660–773):

> I eat a melon
> And think about my children.
> I eat a chestnut
> And think on her I love.
> Whence came they? The vision of them
> Keeps coming before my eyes,
> So that sleep shuns me.

In the *Mannyo Shu* we find the spirit of Japanese antiquity, with its naïve but pure and vigorous polish. It was only by virtue of this spirit that the Japanese were able to adopt the superior culture of the mainland, while still preserving their own spirituality and political independence.

At the beginning of the ninth century Japanese culture experienced its fullest development. Until then Japanese culture had been largely dependent on the Chinese. But in the Hei-an period, with Buddhism fully naturalized in Japan, art was given purely Japanese forms and a corresponding content.

In general the culture of the period is reflected in literature, though this does not always display the highest quality. The best example in the Japanese early Middle Ages is the Hei-an period, which in art history comprises the years between A.D. 795 and 1185. It begins with the removal of the Imperial residence from Nara to Hei-an, the present Kyoto, and ends in 1185 with the fall of the Taira family, which governed Japan for a short time. This period also saw the beginning of critical comparison with foreign culture. In this way the path was opened for the Japanese to a correct understanding of themselves, and their inclination to devote themselves to forming their own creative culture was reinforced.

Two new Buddhist schools, the Shingon sect and the Tendai sect, had their own nationally conditioned points of view. Whereas the Buddhism of the Nara period bore a strongly exegetical character, the new Buddhism tried to get into touch with the people by the way of social welfare. The main stream of art was certainly still preponderantly Buddhist and was particularly closely related to the esoteric school. Of all the Buddhist sects, the esoteric school 'Shingon-Shu', under the leadership of Kobo Daishi (769–831), set the highest value on artistic activity. Besides the two sects, the bearers of culture were the nobility at the Imperial Court led by the Hujiwara family. The nobility, with its power and immeasurable wealth, followed its own bent and created a particularly refined aesthetic way of life, often in complete disregard of morals, ethics, and religion[26]. This one-sided development of the aristocracy brought with it material refinement and emotional sentimentality. The tone was not, as in the preceding age, marked by the vigorous and virile, but by charm and femininity. The liberation from foreign culture and the consequent maturing of the native genius constituted one of the most important characteristics of the Japanese people and did much to promote the development of artistic originality. The same phenomenon can be observed in the Tokugawa period, when the country was shut off from the rest of the world. The basic characteristics of Hei-an art are aristocratic sensualism side by side with exalted naturalism and realism full of feeling and charm.

This basic characteristic of the Japanese art of the central Middle Ages can be particularly well observed in the important novel *The History of Prince Genji*, which was written between 999 and 1011 in fifty-four volumes and is the oldest novel in Japan. It can also be observed in the tendency to the plastic in the Yamato-E school. It is noticeable that in the later years this pure aestheticism of *The*

Tragedy is the expression of nature's innate longing for the Absolute.

History of Prince Genji and the Yamato-E school emerges from a melancholy mood of late summer and autumn—'Mono-no-Aware', as it is called—the ideal of the pure aestheticism of the Hei-an period. The concept of 'Mono-no-Aware' sets the basic mood of Japanese romanticism. In this context the term means the aesthetic atmosphere emanating from life and things. 'Mono-no-Aware' is ultimately the yearning for the primal ground of the eternal. With this idea Murasaki Shikibu (*c.* 978–*c.* 1031), the authoress of *The History of Prince Genji,* character-ized the aesthetic feeling for the inevitability of human fate which had its roots in the outlook on nature and life of esoteric Buddhism. All delight thinks on the eternal. All love yearns for the un-changing. In so far as the idea of the permanent is in-herent in the transitoriness of life, in so far as the feel-ing of everlastingness lies hidden in the search for the eternal, tragedy is the expression of the yearning for the eternal, in other words for the Absolute. Mur-asaki Shikibu, with her fastidiously feminine spirit, describes the course of the love history of the Imperial Prince Genji. It is noteworthy that at this period women were prominent in poetry.

We can perceive this 'Mono-no-Aware' in the following poem by Izimu Shikibu, a lady of the Court:

In the twilight of evening
I am always sad
When I hear the bell.
I do not know
Whether I shall be able to hear it again tomorrow.

Here is a poem by the Buddhist Bishop Henjo (814–890):

O lotus flower, I dreamt the wide earth
Held nothing purer than thee, nothing more true.
But if a dewdrop on thee seems a pearl,
What then of thy purity and truth?

From the ninth century on poetry was an intellectual amusement in the palaces of the great, and at many periods a daily pastime at the Emperor's Court. Poetic mastery secured many liberties for the poet, above all full freedom of speech. To this day a poetic contest takes place at the Imperial Court. In November the theme for the 'New Year's Poem' is announced. Anyone, even the ordinary people, can send in their verses to the Emperor. From these, twenty are selected and read with solemn ceremony in the presence of the Emperor and the entire Court. In the first days of the new year the newspapers publish the names and poems of the winners. It is an event at least as important as a Presidential election or an international football match.

'Yamato-E' is the style of painting which gives

visible expression to the 'Mono-no-Aware' ideal. 'Yamato-E' produced miniature forms, corresponding to its own essence, of the picture scroll, the 'E-Makimono' as it is called. Apparently there were also larger forms of folding screen or sliding door in 'Yamato-E' style. What is certain, however, is that the form of 'E-Makimono' first developed from illustrations of the life of the Buddha. The oldest surviving work on an 'E-Makimono' is the celebrated painting 'The History of Prince Genji'. Four scrolls of this are still extant, relating to thirteen chapters of the book.

In 'E-Makimono' text and illustration are successively arranged in such fashion as to constitute one long scroll, in which the work of art is completed only by the harmony between the two. The work is presumed to date from the first half of the eleventh century and to have been produced by artists of the Imperial Court. The beauty of the colour scheme of the painting depends on its keynote of silver and olive brown, against which blue, green and occasionally red can be distinguished by way of contrast. Just as the novel marks the high point of the national literature then in its flower, the painting represents the perfection of 'Yamato-E'; and it can certainly be assumed that this masterpiece was not without predecessors.

Two hundred years later 'Mono-no-Aware' developed into 'Yugen'. 'Yugen' stands for greater profundity and power of suggestion than does 'Mono-no-Aware'. It looks not only for outward earthly beauty of actual form, but even more for what lies hidden behind it. The Japanese mentality does not, like Heidegger, seek 'clarification of the hidden', but penetration into what is hidden and transformation within it. That is how the essence of nature and of man is reached. In the 'Yugen' concept, 'Yu' means 'mysterious' and 'Gen' means 'skill'. The spirit of 'Yugen' is in other words 'spiritual depth-existence'. The following poem speaks of penetrating into the hiddenness of the evocative:

> The evening hour;
> An autumn wind from the field
> Pierces deep into my heart;
> And quails cry
> In the thickets of Hukagusa.

HUJIWARA NO TOSHINARI (1114–1204)

The following poem was written by the priest Saigyo:

> Swept away by the flood
> How abandoned I feel,
> Alone on the high sea.
> No rescuing vessel is in sight.

42

In the thirteenth century begins a new epoch in the cultural and spiritual history of Japan. Minamoto no Yoritomo (1145–1195), the head of the Minamoto family, was the first to take the title of 'Sei-I-Daishogun' (generalissimo or Imperial field-marshal) and established the seat of his military government at Kamakura (east central Japan). Accordingly the Kamakura culture reflected the military spirit of the age, in complete contrast to the fastidious taste of the Hei-an period. Indeed, the Japanese spirit of chivalry, 'Bushido' as it is called, though it had its origin in far earlier times, took on its own permanent form under Yoritomo. Bushido is the art of illuminating and doing away with the gap between life and death.

This spirit the Japanese knight acquired on the field of battle. Zen Buddhism gave it its metaphysical and religious bases. The well-bred Japanese has a technique for transcending death in the hour of death and seeing it objectively. Often, before dying, he writes a few poems bidding farewell to earthly existence, in which he expresses in brief his ideas about life. Anyone not of this mind is reckoned a barbarian. The Japanese may perhaps have no peculiar philosophy of life: he certainly has a philosophy of death. 'Bushido' is the philosophy of death practised in life. In it there is no difference

between life and death. Sooner than live in dis-
honour, the Japanese dies of his own free will. That
is the principle of the Japanese knightly ethic. The
sword is the symbol of the knight—not merely a
weapon, but a symbol of inner purity.

As we have already observed, in the Kamakura
period art stood in a close relationship to contemporary Buddhism. While the two sects, Tendai and
Shingon, continued to enjoy their traditional
authority, other sects appeared and introduced a
new direction into Japanese religion. It was then
that Japan entered its reformation period. Beside
Zen Buddhism there arose the Jodo sect. Both
gained ground mainly in the countryside and
ministered to the enlightenment of the common
people. Conformably with the spirit of the time,
the teachings of the new sects were simple, clear,
and practical. Generally speaking, too, the consciousness of individuality was considerably developed during the Kamakura period. Fervid personal
veneration of the founders of the sects was a marked
and outstanding feature, and illustrated biographies
of them were written. Portraiture is the distinguish-
ing mark of the period, and with it the religious
limitations of Buddhist art were transcended.

Notable works of art were created by Buddhist
sculptors at Nara, Kyoto, and Kamakura. Of all

these, the school represented by Unkei (died A.D. 1223) particularly distinguished itself. It strove to express virile strength, created many massive memorials, and professed the new realism. The spirit of the time is clearly indicated by the twin statues of 'Mujaku' and 'Seijin', two guardian gods in the 'Kohukuji' temple at Nara. This was the supreme flowering-time of Japanese sculpture. Inevitably, too, the practical aim of bringing religious ideas to the people produced great changes in the art of the period. Buddhist art as earlier understood went into a decline and after the Kamakura period finally disappeared. It now manifested itself in the painting and sculpture bearing the stamp of the new Buddhism. The expression lost its feminine tenderness and became almost hard. In composition and in the management of line the dynamic occupied an ever greater place, lines became thicker and stronger and colours more full of contrast.

The representation of nature in the Kamakura period is to be seen most clearly in the 'E-Makimono' picture scroll. A particular contribution to art of the Kamakura period consisted in portrait painting, which originated in veneration for the founders of the new religion and for warrior heroes, but in addition was promoted by the individualistic

45

spirit of the age and the realistic trend of its art. The portraits of Minamoto no Yoritomo, which have from ancient times been preserved at Jingu-Ji in Kyoto, may be ascribed to Hujiwara no Takanobu, the master of portraiture of the Kamara period. The figure is seated on a mat in black court dress, and is very carefully, but powerfully, depicted. Yoritomo's face has such a living effect that it is easy to discern the personality of the most powerful politician of his time and the founder of the rule of generals.

I would like to give some further attention to the characteristic qualities of the Kamakura period. The aim was to give expression to power. The principal object of Zen Buddhism is to render power absolute by means of the practice of Zen meditation. Zen exercise is the art of the soul consisting in emptying oneself completely and at the same time rendering oneself absolute. This dialectic contrast is unmistakably a spiritual phenomenon of Japan. Clear lines and powerful brush-strokes now became the aesthetic expression of this spirit. In this period the whole cultural level was raised. Five monastic universities were founded at Kyoto and five in Kamakura, together with two independent universities in east Japan—Kanagawa-Bunko and Ashikaga-Gakko—of which St. Francis Xavier later gave an account.

The Muromachi period involved a new and important turning-point in the whole of Japanese art. The period opened with the establishment at Kyoto of the new 'Sei-I-Daishogun' by Ashikaga Takanji (he also came from the Minamoto family) in A.D. 1338, and ended with the overthrow of the last Generalissimo Ahikaga Yoshiaki by the newly arisen soldier prince Oda Nobinaga in A.D. 1573. The late Muromachi period corresponds to the renaissance in Italy, and was influenced by the spirit of the new age. In this period the seat of government was moved from Kamakura to Kyoto, and so the political and culture centre were once more united.

The third Generalissimo Yoshimitsu (1356–1407) had built a palace—known as the 'Flower Palace'—in Muromachi, a quarter of Kyoto, and to the north-west of Kyoto the villa 'Gold Pavilion' (1397). In magnificence of display and luxury of living he followed the example of the Hujiwara family, and all his successors did the same. The peak of this epoch was the Higashiyama period. The eighth Generalissimo Yoshimasa (1433–1489) had a magnificent palace built to the east of Kyoto on the Higashiyama mountain: in its garden, Ginkaku-Ji (the 'Silver Pavilion') was erected in 1483. In this beautiful and tranquil landscape, surrounded by artists, he found his peace. This was the so-called

47

'Higashiyama' art, which not only took the first steps in a new artistic direction, but also was extremely important for the modern Japanese style of living. The Higashiyama period was the turning-point in the history of Japanese culture. At its central point stood the development of the art of 'Cha-no-yu', the tea ceremony, which was brought to perfection by Seno no Rikyu (1520–1591).

But what is this 'tea ceremony'? It is called 'Chado', that is, 'the way and the essence of tea'. It is the way that every educated Japanese must follow; it is reality become a symbol of the depths of Japanese spirituality. The Japanese always conceives of art as a way, as the goal of spiritual yearning and also as the norm of human life. This norm is not merely the external form of art, but also the inward destination of human life. The essence of the tea ceremony has no outwardly attainable goal. Its form and its practice offer no more than hints. The process of learning the tea art, which calls for no specified period of tuition, and so requires years or even a whole lifetime in order to attain the final steps of absorption, is an endless way which yet leads to no end. What distinguishes this ceremony from all other arts or ethical acts is that in it man has himself for object. Man as a corporeal and spiritual unity grows as a whole into the work of art by virtue of his natural peculiarities and qualities. He works on himself both as artist and as subject. The heightening of all the senses, the deepening of the powers of spirit and psyche, occur in him as it were spontaneously. Commonplace as it is in terms of human activity, the tea ceremony requires no departure from life and reality. It is not contempt for the world, neither does it know anything of ecstasy. It seeks only that primal human basic consciousness which is unconscious consciousness.

The tea room is only nine or twelve square yards in area, and in it all those present conceal their individual education and class in mutual respect and enjoy each other's society in calm and serenity. No distinction is made between noble, professor, and peasant. In the tea room equality rules. Age alone implies authority, and the only distinction is that between host and guests. At the tea ceremony the use of colloquial speech is banned on principle. The maximum possible taciturnity is required, and such exchanges of speech as are permitted must be couched in poetic form and in the most distinguished style. Conversation of this kind is proper to the tea activity. Each answers according to his attainments, and speaks of the conquest of the dualism between the I and the world, finitude and eternity, appearance and essence, good and bad,

49

subject and object. The art of tea is a philosophical exercise.

The art of tea concerns not only tea drinking and the art of cookery, or the hanging picture and flower arrangement—both of them arts contributing to the adornment of the tea room—but has also created its own norms in architecture and gardening. The costume of those taking part in the tea ceremony accords with the spirit of the prescribed refinement of taste. It is, in fact, the object of the tea ceremony to discover an aesthetic style of living in every sphere of life.

Higashiyama art was an important synthetic art with a bearing on Japanese life. In the arts and crafts, which were closely connected with the tea cere-mony, the development of pottery was specially noteworthy. In the fields of lacquer and gold-smith's work there were many masters. Goto Yujyo (1440–1512) and Koami Michinaga (1410–1478) were the most important representatives of Higashiyama artistic circles. These artists all came from the circle of friends about Generalissimo Yoshimasa or his Court. In domestic architecture there arose a new style, the so-called 'Sho-in-Zukuri'. This new way of building developed very rapidly. It is the foundation of the general style of living in Japan at the present day.

The essential features of Higashiyama art, extending into all fields, can be summarized in one word in the idea of 'Wabi', which is supposed to express the highest beauty and can also be carried over into other fields of art. Fundamentally it means poverty, and at the same time simplicity and calm, but it also implies an inexpressible inner joy hidden deep in modesty. That is the basic principle of the tea art. Out of 'Wabi' developed harmony, respect, purity, poverty—harmony of colour, form, light, touch, movement; respect for the guest, for oneself, for nature; purity of soul, purity of space, purity of the world; poverty of man, poverty of nature.

That is what the special designation of 'Wabi' amounts to: it was the favourite expression of the Haiku masters, and we shall go into it again later.

It was this artistic atmosphere that saw the rise of the master Seami (1353–1444), who in this period developed the No theatre—symbolic drama—and gave it its artistic perfection. Painting, too, had a symbolic character in this period. The most important painter was the priest Sesshu (1419–1506). In his works the line is in general strong, broad, very sure, and full of power: their beauty is incomparable. These characteristics constitute the sincerity and tension of his work, the peculiar quality of

Sesshu (1419 - 1506)

which rests on the clarity of his conception: this
enabled him to apprehend the essential immediately
and then to render it with economy of form. The
only colours he used were black and white. From
his works it is easy to perceive that he painted
'Wabi' experience. His art appears to be nothing
other than the expression of the psychic absorption
attained by means of Zen Buddhism.

In this connection, garden art is particularly
worthy of mention. This took its rise in the central
Middle Ages in the Hei-an period (ninth to twelfth
centuries), but was perfected as an art in the
Higashiyama period. Garden art is an entirely
special art. Its materials are rock, water, and trees
which have been subjected to the changes imposed
by time. The garden artist must first of all endeavour to give a living and harmonious unity to the
changing object and at the same time to provide
for the harmony of form to be assumed in the
future. In every season, in every year, in every
generation, the garden displays contrasts and harmonies of varied forms and colours. Mere nature
is not nature in its purity: the impure must be kept
away from it in order to yield its primal purity of
form. This creation of the spirit ranks as the art of
harmony in change.

Another important development was Renga

poetry, which had a close relationship with the tea ceremony. One person composes a half-stanza and someone else has to complete the poem. For example, one man wrote the following second half:

> I would willingly have averted it,
> But I could not.

> SOKAN [27]

Three different people added the first half in three different ways. The first was a father vacillating between justice and mercy. He wrote:

> A thief was taken by night
> And, when lights were brought,
> I recognized my son.

> SOKAN

Another participant in the game chose a realistic interpretation and made the following addition:

> Through a grievous mishap
> My left arm was sadly injured
> And causes me bitter pain.

> AN UNKNOWN GUEST OF SOKAN

A third, more emotionally, wrote:

> Through the dense boughs of a plum-tree
> I looked up and saw the moon.
> Then the glowing face was hidden
> By a sheltering branch.

> AN UNKNOWN GUEST OF SOKAN

The year 1539 brought an important political event in Japanese history: the first Europeans came to Japan. This event, however, had scarcely any significance for the history of Japanese art. In order to pursue the history of Japanese art further, it is necessary to treat of the period following the Momoyama period. One of the most celebrated works of this period is the fresco in the Chishaku-In temple in Kyoto, painted by the master Hasegawa Tohoku in 1609. This work in its style of expression is typical of the period. In it figure ornamental plants, arranged in accordance with the four seasons on a gold-coloured background on sliding doors and tapestries. The peak of the sequence of paintings is constituted by two scenes with cherry blossom and red maple. It can be designated, not only as regards materials, but also in its conception of form, as fully characteristic of Japanese art.

In this period, in the year 1549, the Japanese for the first time made contact with Christianity, but this found few adherents. There were several reasons:

1. The lack of agreement between the governing ways of thinking about spiritual matters peculiar to Europeans and Japanese.

2. Resistance to European colonialism. It was unfortu-

nate that the first Christian mission was very closely connected with the power of Spain and Portugal.

3. The extreme conservative policy of the current military régime and the radical, militaristic spirit of the period.

4. The failure of the new religion to produce more than a handful of indigenous priests to carry it on, whereas the Buddhist mission of the fifth and sixth centuries A.D. had quickly secured numerous adherents.

5. The excessive ruthlessness of the missionary methods employed by the Catholic missionary orders, and the struggle for power between those orders themselves.

For these reasons Christianity, though it had spread rapidly at the outset, was eventually prohibited by the Japanese government in 1638. Toyotomi Hideyoshi (1534–1596), a great warrior, was the ruler of Japan at this epoch. The spirit of the Momoyama period exactly reflected his character. He was active and powerful, but at the same time liberal-minded. By virtue of his military and political power he shaped a new generation. Possessed as he was of incalculable wealth and enormous power, he built huge castles, citadels, and temples everywhere.

The Momoyama period was followed by the Tokugawa period. Fundamentally the art of the early

Tokugawa period was the successor to the school of Momoyama art. From this period art freed itself progressively from religious ties. The basic character of the early Tokugawa period bore the impress of realism and naturalism. In form it was very faithful to nature, yet decorative as well.

In the middle Tokugawa period art attained its supreme flowering. The Tokugawa period began in 1603 and lasted till 1868. Peace prevailed for 250 years under the Tokugawa military régime. At the beginning of the period the military spirit still held firm, but after half a century it slowly and progressively became absorbed in the political order. Social life saw the rise of the middle class, particularly in Kyoto, Osaka, and Edo. In literary creation the modern trend and the popular element gained strength, as can be seen from the field of the novel in Saikaku (1642–1694), of the drama of Chikamatsu (1653–1724), and of Haiku poetry in Basho (1653–1694).

Very much the same process was repeated in the plastic arts. One name became the epitome of the age—that of Ogata Korin (1657–1716). He came of a wealthy merchant family in Kyoto and from his early years was instructed in the arts of the tea ceremony, the No play, and Haiku poetry, as far as possible indeed in all contemporary arts and general culture. In conformity with the Japanese ideal of culture, he was successful in the most varied arts and attained to a high degree of mastery, particularly in ornamental lacquer work.

His works of art are highly ornamental. One of his most important pieces is 'Irises', painted on a six-sided pair of folding screens (Nezu Museum, Tokyo). On the large panels figure nothing but irises on a golden background. Korin's principal subject was the world of plants. The Momoyama period saw the development of plant and bird painting, representing the intimacy and calm of classicism: in the Tokugawa period it found perfection at the hands of Korin.

European ideas made scarcely any impact on Japanese art. This was rooted in a view of the world and a mode of perception quite different from those of Europe. In contrast to the European, the Japanese objective way of looking at nature proceeds from the subjective and temperamental, and yet seeks, and stylizes, the irregular. The principle of the decorative style is an asymmetrical, irregular order.[28] This is to be seen most clearly in Korin's decorative painting. Japanese painting seems in his work to have attained the final step in its development.

With the late Tokugawa period (1730–1868)

began a great new phase of artistic creation in so many different directions as to make very difficult any uniform characterization. The most important art-form is the Haiku poem of only seventeen syllables. The greatest master of his time was Matsuo Basho (1643–1694). In Basho we encounter immediately the Japanese world of experience, which hitherto had never been properly based on pure theory and is summed up in the idea of 'Sabi'. The idea of 'Sabi' is closely akin to the idea of 'Wabi', as has already been mentioned, but it is less aesthetic. By the idea of 'Sabi' the Japanese understands such concepts as solitude, tranquillity, poverty, and simplicity. 'Sabi' cannot be analysed conceptually. The 'Sabi' experience resembles the experience of 'satori' in Zen. Basho expresses this experience in the following poem:

> Summer grass
> Is all that remained
> Of old soldiers' dreams.

Here is another poem:

> On a dead bough
> Sits a crow
> At nightfall in autumn.

Most of his poems are enigmatic and mysterious; in seventeen syllables he points to the mysterious world. The economical use of words produces in poetry the effect of implication—one of the secrets of Japanese art.

Basho was a forerunner of the late Tokugawa period. Taking its pattern from him there developed a new trend in painting, the expressionism of the Nan-ga school side by side with the naturalism of the Maruyama school, which adapted itself as closely as possible to the realistic mood of the times. Both revealed the spirit of the age in the clearest possible way. The masters of the Nan-ga school were for the most part also masters of Haiku poetry. The greatest of them were Yosa Buson (1716–1783) and Ike no Jaiga (1723–1776). The form is free and full of rich artistic fantasy, the colour scheme light, dreamy and soft, despite its keynote of black. The motif is always something supernatural. Buson's most important poem is the following:

> On the temple bell,
> Sleeping,
> A butterfly.

Side by side with the Nan-ga school the Maruyama school was thriving in Kyoto: this school developed the realistic trend of Momoyama painting into naturalism. Maruyama Okyo (1723–1795) the founder of the school that bears his name, must on account of this naturalism be recognized as a painter of world standard. On the other hand, it is undeniable that he set great store by colour harmony. This tendency seems to derive from the tradition of Japan, the more so since it was that of Kyoto. Okyo opened a new path for Japanese art. Okyo is noted for sure management of the brush, intelligent composition, and objective observation.

Other cultural fields were at that time dominated by realism. Motoori Nohinaga (1717–1801) studied philology scientifically, and indicated a new direction for the spirit of the Japanese nation.[29]

Another art of this period is the woodcut. The Ukiyo-E woodcut of Edo is a synthesis of the expressionism of the Nan-ga school with the realism of the Maruyama school. Its flowering time came at the end of the Tokugawa period, and it was then supreme among the fine arts. The painters merely made preliminary sketches for woodcuts: a few did produce paintings, it is true, but their value at first was slight. The artistic importance of the woodcut grew ever greater. The colour print was not intended as a reproduction of a painting. The favourite themes of Ukiyo-E are women and girls from the market stalls and scenes from ordinary life: pictures of actors are quite rare. The inclina-

Sesshu is admitted by Japanese connoisseurs as his country's greatest painter;
particularly its greatest painter of landscape. His life and his art bear the stamp
of Zen. When we look at his picture, we forget the conditions of space and
time which we can establish in all other Zen paintings. In this picture he
employs the Haboku method (technique of cursive wash) in order to bring the
majestic power of nature to immediate expression for nature is the body of
the Buddha. This picture represents the eyes of nature, which flows in the
water The eyes draw all existence through the various dimensions down to
the depths of the ultimate ground

In Sesshu's works the line is in general very strong, broad and sure The
handling of the brush is powerful and free. This tightness of composition and
simplicity of colour rendering are the complementary expression of the Zen
experience. The eyes of nature are situated in the centre of the picture Presumably the subject derives from one of the Zen koans (themes of Zen
meditation) which seek the experience of the absolute in the resolution
of paradox

Shubun was a priest of the Shokoku-Ji Zen monastery in Kyoto He was a pupil of Nyosetsu but far surpassed his master In Zen landscape painting there are three rules of style for distant views·

1. Distant and high A view upward from below.

2 Distant and deep A view from foreground to background

3 Distant and shallow A view from near at hand to far away

In this picture Shubun presents distant views which hint at the other world In this way the impression of the infiniteness of the mysterious landscape is enhanced and the beholder plunges into the inmost essence of nature The little boat by the shore gives the feeling of absolute solitude

Sesson was not a direct pupil of Sesshu, but he was one of his greatest followers. In this picture he employs masterly force and powerful brushwork to depict the growth of harmony in spring. In the foreground is the broad expanse of water, in the middle distance the fragrance of the blossoming plum tree, and in the background the spiritualized mountain wreathed in cloud. This is a projection of the landscape of the soul

Nothing precise is known about the life of Koko He is assumed to have been a Zen priest in Kyoto and to have lived about the fifteenth century

In this picture the mountain landscape by the sea is treated with gentle brushwork and tranquil composition The house at the mountain foot forms the centre of the picture Here we find the concord of heaven and earth, and penetrate deep into the Nothing Several tea masters have found their life ideal in this picture

Earnestness of mood and purity of soul attained through Zen exercises, manifest themselves in this scene of nature depicted in light colours and simple technique The poem written at the top reads as follows

Behind the house is a high mountain
From the shore the blue sea goes on
    for thousands of miles.
Now a ship sails, somewhither
In the descending moonlight
    the bells are heard at dead of night

tion for realism brought with it this ordinariness of scene, sometimes with an emphasis on vulgar sensuality—as well might be appropriate to the essence of Ukiyo-E. Another element enters in, endowing reality with something dreamlike. It is undoubtedly due to fineness of line, softness of colour, stillness of pose, and a manner of composition by virtue of which even the spaces left vacant by the cutting acquire something of the intimacy of an inner room.[30] All this is particularly marked in the work of Suzuki Harunobu (1724–1770). What is fundamental is generalization accompanied by refinement of taste—a characteristic feature of Japanese art. The greatness of Harunobu's achievement is demonstrated by his ingenious adaptation to the particular exigencies of the woodcut. Technically he was the most highly gifted master of the Ukiyo-E woodcut.

In the first half of the nineteenth century Ukiyo-E made advances in colour-printing technique. At this time aniline was discovered. Painters of this period who should be mentioned are Katsushika Kokusai (1760–1849), Utagawa Toyokuni (1769–1825), Ando Hiroshige (1796–1858), and Kitagawa Utamaro (1753–1806). The names of these artists are well known in Europe, many of their works having been sent there.

To the Japanese mind Ukiyo-E art is imperfect, despite its successful composition of line and colour. It lacks idealism, which is an essential feature of Japanese art. For that reason it is admired by the Japanese rather than revered. Unfortunately it was the first to become known in Europe, so that the European impression of Japanese art is quite one-sided.

The value of the culture of modern Japan cannot be assessed from the objective historical standpoint alone, nor can it be set in its place in the country's spiritual history. Art is a reflected image of the human soul and requires distance if the picture is to be seen properly. Accordingly the last century cannot be taken into consideration.

V

CATEGORIES OF JAPANESE ART [31]

THE EUROPEAN way of thinking and living, with the tensions that characterize it —between the exterior and the interior world, the natural and the spiritual world, object and subject, object of knowledge and consciousness—stands in sharp contrast to the Japanese life of the spirit. Such tensions are unknown to the Japanese: rather there is a state of correspondence between the two poles. [32]

Buddhism, which raised the nature doctrine of Shintoism to the level of a metaphysic, says: All things are as they seem—they do not possess genuine being, only appearance. A further teaching is: Everything is unstable and subject to change, and only when the self returns to the higher Self is truth perceived, attained, and experienced.

The beautiful is the vital principle of the cosmos. The light of the stars, the sight of flowers in bloom or of clouds soaring in the sky, the humour of the

[handwritten margin note: How is this not world-denying?]

ordinary man—such are the things in which the cosmos mirrors itself. This correspondence between nature and spirit dominates the artistic and spiritual history of Japan.

The human relation of all beings to the Nothing shows itself first of all through the 'DO', the 'way'. The idea of the 'way' connotes 'an endless striving to enter the Absolute'. Among the common people these ideas are to be found only in the form of a free creative capacity and a profound insight into all possible objects.

Such a mental attitude towards the rest of the world must express itself unmistakably in the artistic style of the people. It is evident that everything in the world, its whole organic and vital structure, is inwardly connected and mutually related. It would be possible to see in the work of art a world sufficient to itself in this universal connectedness. Man, however, habitually sees reality, not in its pure form, but in accordance with his own peculiar mode of being which identifies him as existing in space and history. If a piece of nature is so represented in a work of art that the thing represented breathes the 'dimension' of aesthetic reality illustrated by the world, the 'dimension' of reality in the true sense of the word, then the creator of the work merits the name of master. These 'dimensional qualities' of aesthetic reality condition the categories existing in all spheres of Japanese art. In this sense aesthetic reality is the true form of the cosmos.

Whereas in Europe great importance is attached to the outer form and inner self-sufficiency of a work of art, in Japan things are the other way round. There the centre of gravity lies in the formless art within, and its categories—its basic ideas—are 'limitlessness', 'unfinishedness', and 'naturalness'. We might well be surprised that two such opposed ways of basic behaviour and thought can exist in one and the same human race. We may hope, on closer consideration that both roads will in the end lead to the same goal. The European idea of the world—rational, constructive, and concerned with space and extension as it is—finds common reality so obtrusive that the artist tries as far as possible to express his work and himself within a definite framework and to remove them from that reality, in order that they may exist in the ideal aesthetic world of art—in the reality of art in the true sense of the word. The Japanese, on the contrary, is more concerned with the artistic process than with the finished work. This—the work—is an expression of an artistic process, and when contemplated, is experienced simultaneously by participation and by following through.[33]

Categories of Japanese Art

A people like the Japanese, with their dislike for
the exclusion of the spiritual, had to experience their
ideal aesthetic world in the things of every day. The
artist cared very little whether his work was influenced by the harsh reality of practical life. Logic-
ally enough, the Japanese have abolished the
boundaries between art and life. Their everyday
habits and gestures, all their conditions of living,
must be art. In the narrower sense art is only a part
of the art of living.[34] Consequently any given object
of daily use is artistically formed, and applied art
acquires another and a more significant place in art
than it does in Europe. Moreover, the individual
arts approach one another more closely or even
merge, so that the frontiers between them are, so to
speak, effaced. Beside the art of tea stand lacquer
work, flower arrangement, architecture, gardening,
cookery. . . . But all these are subordinated to the
tea ceremony as being the art of living.

The exacting object of Japanese art—to arouse the
active artistic participation of the beholder—has by
way of consequence that 'limitlessness' which
assumes various forms in the reality of the artistic
process. Within the category of 'limitlessness' there
are two sub-categories—'unfinishedness' and
'naturalness'.[35] The idea of 'limitlessness' is a metaphysical conception. It implies that art and life are

inseparably fused, that man stands in open opposition to the world of nature and spirit, that art must be considered as a symbol of the totality of the cosmos. This should not be taken to mean that all Japanese works of art were lacking in the quality of being self-contained, still less that Japanese painting knows nothing of frames for its pictures. For this very reason, because Japanese art sees unity in every beautiful thing, there are works which at first sight seem so complete as apparently to refute the proposition concerning 'limitlessness'. The concept of 'limitlessness' on principle rejects an *a priori* and constructive rationalism. The basic quality of 'limitlessness' is 'complementarity', because completeness is less than becoming. This peculiarity characterizes the entire Japanese way of thinking. What is considered by the beholder of art must be understood absolutely as a Something not formulated in formal ways. For example, the white space left in the margin of a picture is more important than the painting itself, at any rate when taken in conjunction with the painted part. The following poem is a good example:

> The old pond:
> A frog jumps in—
> The sound of the water.

MATSUO BASHO

67

This unique verse, made up of four nouns, one adjective and one verb, contains Basho's entire philosophy. An old pond overgrown with reeds, the water stagnant. No one ever comes to this forgotten spot. Suddenly the stillness is broken. What happened? Only a frog jumping in. The life of man is like that. He is just an empty body made of dust: but when he moves, or makes a sound, the life-force can be perceived in him. In that moment of intuition Basho seizes the essence and meaning of human life. The now belongs to eternity. The background is metaphysical. 'Limitlessness', by means of which the inconceivable Something is expressed, points to a certain 'unfinishedness': works of art, self-contained though they may appear to be, are to be looked at as though they were unfinished, or if it is preferred, to be enjoyed as parts, for that is appropriate to the essence of the work of art.

When the artist deliberately represents his object as unfinished the fact holds good in the true sense of the word. 'Unfinishedness' connotes a number of meanings, for example irregularity, incompleteness, asymmetry. . . .

This 'unfinishedness' can assume different forms, according as the art in question permits. At one time the thing represented appears like a given portion of the whole, so that the beholder is summoned to artistic participation in complementary fashion by developing the whole in imagination and, on the basis of what is given, attaining full understanding of it. At another time a living being or a plant is for preference represented incomplete, so that the beholder mentally paints in the missing part and thus inwardly traces the upward-soaring strength of that which lives.

'Limitlessness', the essence of which consists in indicating the infinitely large—namely the world-whole—by comparison with the infinitely small—that is, the object represented, as in garden art—also contains the sub-category of 'naturalness' as an idea complementary to that cosmic totality which has not found its way into art. 'Naturalness' is not a fusion of nature and natural object. This peculiarity distinguishes Japanese art from the Chinese and other ways of perceiving art. 'Naturalness' in turn comprises several divisions, such as intimacy with nature, identity of man and nature, piety of nature, purity of nature—supposing nature lacked purity. In 'naturalness' nature is transformed into art. This means that 'naturalness' is the aesthetic function of nature and art, is both reality and ideal. Its inclination is to disregard the scale of things and to make them still smaller than they really are, because nature is a constant archetype and model for human creative power, but is itself not art. 'Limitlessness' means indeterminacy of forms just where nature is indeterminate in its forms. There is accordingly no formal determinacy, merely expression of inward content. In this sense the beholder must sometimes bring imagination to objects of art and illuminate them in accordance with his own spiritual ability, his degree of human experience and his personal idea of the beautiful. The oftener he undergoes this profound and valuable experience, the better he can comprehend the work of art.

On the other hand, 'naturalness' also contributes to the concentration and deepening of the contemplation of nature. From then onward every object affecting the taste is refined. A dwelling in good taste, even tools that are to work beautifully and honestly, must be 'elegant'. This 'elegance' indicates the relation of the artistic to the infinite microcosm and simultaneously implies development into the infinite macrocosm. Hence a huge building is not a finished whole, but the sum of several elegant works of art and artistic skills. The conditions of life impose elegance on art from outside, and that elegance is an important factor in 'naturalness' and is certainly favoured by 'unfinishedness'. The artist finds his task as a craftsman rendered much more difficult by this 'elegance'. Not only is he to demonstrate his skill, but also he must elevate the idea and at the same time disregard the scale of nature. This principle of elevating and of disregarding the natural scale both constitutes 'unfinishedness' and is also the principle of deepening of artistic activity. Since magnitude is a spatial concept which subsists only on the basis of comparison, natural magnitude cannot in this case afford a valid standard.[36] It is not the standard of art, but the standard of actual reality, and is to be applied only where art chooses nature as its subject and desires to imitate, say, a stretch of landscape in its own spatial setting. Elegance relates above all to the materials of which a work of art is composed, but, as a matter of logic, it also relates to its size. For it is necessary to calculate not only the material and the size which restores all elegance to natural magnitude, but also the harmony of material and size, since the substance consists of plants, rocks, and lumps of earth, and the whole work is a section of a landscape. Hence the smaller is represented as larger, and the larger as smaller, in complementary fashion. Here the world of actual reality collapses, for elegance is a concept of the ideal world.

These categories are symbolic principles of Japanese art. They are valid not only in the sphere of the plastic arts, but also in all other fields of Japanese art.

The nature (essence) of art (
is the art of nature (yūgen – spontaneity)
just-as-it-is-ness

Categories of Japanese Art

From closer consideration of the basic concept of 'limitlessness', with its sub-categories of 'unfinished-ness' and 'naturalness', it can be perceived that 'unfinishedness' means a movement in the direction of infinity and goes back to Buddhist influence, whilst 'naturalness' in its turn is something innate in the Japanese people, an artistic reflection of its own self. 'Limitlessness' is the synthesis in which the two are merged and complete one another.

unfinishedness – Buddhist

naturalness – Japanese

Limitlessness – Synthesis of both

VI

SOME CHARACTERISTICS OF
JAPANESE ART [37]

IN SO far as Japanese art concerns itself with representing the essence of nature and the spirit, it returns home, as it were. It is evident that 'limitlessness' is well adapted for giving form to nature by means of art. Following his bent, the Japanese immerses himself in nature and thereby abolishes the boundaries between himself and the world. For him there exists only the higher nature, the Nothing, as ground and primal origin of being, which also includes man.

Plastic art is directed on the one hand towards the representation of anything and everything objective, on the other hand towards the expression of the inner or subjective. There is no objective delineation in artistic activity. This becomes the problem in the case both of artistic creation and of contemplation of art. Since the manner of representing the one and the ideal fashion of expressing the other spring from quite different origins, many different artistic schools arise, which, consonantly with the spirit of the times, reflect the peculiar character of a nation or even of an individual. Japanese art sets more store by profound inner expression than by representation of the objective, as witness the art of tea, the art of gardening and flower arrangement, which are pure arts of expression.

That Japanese art in its mode of expression leans rather to symbolism than to realism and naturalism, and also firmly rejects individualism, is clearly established by its tendency to typify.[38] This tendency is clearly marked in the Ukiyo-E woodcuts. It is nothing other than a generalization of art-forms. The psychological basis of artistic creation is different from that prevailing in Europe. For the Japanese, the development and assertion of his own individuality as the first principle of art has less value than for the European. The most important thing is rather individual development into general primal forms, and the highest aim of art is absorption in the super-individual.[39] It is, therefore, intelligible that a firm attachment to tradition is to be observed in the development of Japanese art as a special phenomenon. This is manifested in the development of several schools which in all fields of art—literature, swordsmanship, the tea ceremony—

have been carried on by a few particular families from one generation to another ever since the Middle Ages. In painting the Kano and the Tosa schools were prominent, in the tea ceremony the Zen school, in swordsmanship the Yagui school, in poetry the Nidyo family, which belonged to the highest nobility, and so on.

For Japanese artists, therefore, decadence hardly poses a problem. What matters first, in all fields of art, is to learn the 'primary form' and to attain complete command of it. This 'primary form' is the original, generalized prototype which has been laid down and defined as the basic form by several earlier masters. In this form there is no room for individualism. That is the firmly established principle of Japanese art. If a man attains full command of this primary form and then on the basis of it proceeds to develop a form of his own, he is a complete master. Only the master creates his own individual style. It is not permitted to repeat the art-form, but in art training repetition is the first principle.

Art is related not only to an intellectual Something which can be comprehended by means of formal thought and analytic perception, but rather to the entire human personality in which a unity is created by feeling, will, and reason.

So far as concerns abstract art, which in modern times makes such lofty claims, the Japanese appreciates it as an art still in the future. Abstract art lays strong emphasis on the expression of the individual parts, but it lacks the absolutely essential principle in accordance with which these are set in order. Art is not subordinated to human arbitrariness. There is a definite and rigid law, as, for instance, that of complementarity, for expressing the representation of a part. This law is rooted deep in the primal consciousness of mankind. Abstract art is only a particular phenomenal form and an experiment regarding which nothing definitive can yet be said.

The essence of our art has its roots deep in the peculiar character of the people and in the Buddhist outlook on the world. It lays stress on simplicity of form, economy of line and softness of colour. These are the consequences flowing from a progressive refinement of feeling. A cry, a brush-stroke, even a gesture of a finger, are capable of expressing an emotion unlimited in content.[40] For the understanding of a set of facts which are beyond explanation and logic, intuition is particularly used in Japanese art as a suitable medium. In addition, silent communication 'from soul to soul' is highly valued. How economical is the use of words in Haiku

poetry! How taciturn is the tea ceremony! This is a
characteristic of Japanese art and Japanese life.

In this connection there follows a further problem—that of the value by world standards of
Japanese art,[41] the question whether Japanese art is
simply an imitation of Chinese, and whether, if so,
it still possesses general validity for the world and
can be rightly understood by other nations. There is
no doubt that Japanese art took its models from the
Asiatic continent. The strongest proof of this is
afforded by the Imperial collection, already mentioned, in the treasury at Shoso-In at Nara, which
dates from the year 756. It should, moreover, not be
overlooked that our ancestors took every oppor-
tunity of adopting suggestions from abroad. As a
result of adopting foreign elements, Japanese art lost
a good deal of its primitive form. We Japanese are
sufficiently modest to give serious attention to
studying things of the spirit from foreign lands, and
then to master them and carry them further. We
have, therefore, always set before us the task of
orienting foreign elements towards our own primal
essence and of raising them to the level of genuine
art. Thus it was only in Japan that tea drinking,
taken over from China, was developed into a true
art. Subsequently the art of tea became something
more than a mere refinement of the custom of tea

77

drinking: with us it is the completion of the art of living.

The second question we cannot answer, because we Japanese have no right to do so. The answer must be given by the other national cultures. In the last hundred years, however, impressionist painters in France, like Cézanne, Monet, Manet, Toulouse-Lautrec, and Van Gogh, have drawn inspiration from the peculiar motifs and delicate colour schemes of Japanese painting,[42] just as architects and landscape gardeners, particularly in America, have received a powerful impetus from Japanese art from the point of view of light and space effects. They have opened a new world to modern art, though that still leaves unanswered the question how far they have been able really to appreciate the essence of Japanese art. Nevertheless, we may be permitted to say that Japanese art is at least a possible development of art generally, and has played an important role for mankind, even though it has never yet been a determining factor in the main streams of the art of the world.

VII

'DO' AS WAY AND ESSENCE OF ART [43]

FOR THE Japanese, art is the way to the Absolute and to the essence of human life. This he designates as 'DO'. This way is not to be described, but to be walked, and it indicates the sole possibility of artistic creation. 'DO' is infinite, undetermined, and unlimited, yet it is the constant goal of spiritual yearning and striving. The cultural history of Japan is nothing other than an endless way which is situated in reality, but ends in infinity. However far the traveller goes, his end remains ever on the horizon. Art is an eternal way that can never be completed, and finds neither satiety nor fulfilment.

The nature of 'DO' cannot be conceptually defined. We can only represent the sort of thing it is. All attempts at such a definition are relative. Confucius said, 'If I understood "DO" in the morning,

death might come in the evening.' For the majority
of mankind, death is generally the end, and the
conclusion of a once-for-all existence spent in
triviality, an existence in which the way that was
sought—'DO'—has not been found. Despite the
contradiction with comprehensible reality, 'DO'
can penetrate the horizon of experience. In other
words, by means of rigid and uninterrupted self-
control and self-conquest, 'DO' can be existentially
grasped in a marginal experience which breaks
through the wall of the finite to reach infinity. Then,
in place of dreamlike fantasy and the thought-forms
of the intellect, there enters an uplifting power of
self-command and refinement of the forms of
experience. The essence of Japanese spiritual crea-
tions is rooted in this unfathomable source, deep in
the ground of the transcendent cosmic law and of
the immanent consciousness of the inward man.

The Japanese spirit has little liking for extension
in space or formation in time: rather it rejects so
far as possible all external, natural magnitude, which
ensnares the spirit and hands it over in its material
quality to transitoriness.[44] Everything human that
appears to have form in space is conditioned by
time, even though it stands firm for thousands of
years. The artistic experience has no basis in the
external work, even when the spirit gives it form in

actuality, but only in the essence of eternity itself. In order to penetrate the essence of the eternal, everything spatio-temporal, everything transitory, everything that ultimately decays, must be stripped away. Penetration into 'DO' and transformation into 'DO' constitute the ultimate goal of Japanese art and the Zen in the art of living.

The 'DO' consists in the ultimate, inner cosmic experience which shapes the self: it is reality become the symbol of Japanese psychic life. In the 'DO' the spiritual history of the Far East, and particularly of Japan, appears like a living work of art, complete and sublime, and free for several thousand years past of the fetters of the rationalism to come. Before the profundity of the 'DO' every system of philosophy is silent: in face of the 'DO'-soul all poetry and all literature is dumb.

I would like at this point to indicate ten steps in the experience of truth[45] in the 'DO':

1. Seeking and striving after truth.

    Physiological, psychological, physical, etc. Mastery of all human capacities by means of exercise and study, learning and repetition, with a view to grasping everything essential. Complete elimination of the inessential.

2. Awareness of truth.

    In order to become aware of truth, a definite

attitude of mind is required, and this must be acquired through training. Under the guidance of the master this training consists in liberation from cosmic laws.

3. Perception of truth.

Once truth is felt, it is possible by means of further training and effort to attain a definite spiritual dimension in which it is possible to perceive what truth is.

4. Understanding of truth.

Man lives and works in the truth, wishes and acts within the framework of the truth. A passive retention in reality of comprehension of the truth. When the Something is oriented in the Nothing, it is true.

5. Experiencing truth.

Creation out of the truth. The experience of truth is a creative process. The shapeless acquires shape, the formless form. An active mastery of truth in reality.

6. Mastering truth.

The man who experiences truth creatively turns back on himself and finds the truth in himself. Consciousness of truth no longer exists. The further the understanding goes, the simpler things are.

7. Forgetting truth.

With the return to and immersion in oneself,

there is no truth any more. Man finds himself as a carrier of truth in the primal consciousness.

8. Forgetting the carrier of truth.
   Consciousness no longer exists. In the primal consciousness the self as carrier of truth forgets and disappears.

9. Return to the primal source where truth has its roots.
   That is, the self and the primal consciousness, the ground of the self, disappear, and man stands over against the Nothing.

10. Repose in the Nothing.

All Japanese arts must mount unswervingly by these steps.

The way of the tea ceremony, the 'Cha-DO', explains this series of steps clearly.[46]

The entrance to the tea room is narrow and low, not more than three feet high. In following this way all must learn humility. Before the ceremony proper begins, mouth and hands are cleansed. The action begins with cordial greetings outside, and ends with the guests bowing low in farewell and watching the host clearing everything away. Nothing is left in the room—except the room's emptiness. In the room there is never anything superfluous. The end is performed in exactly the same fashion as the beginning. There is no climax accompanied by

83

flights into the empyrean.[47] 'As a white cloud floats
away in the clear sky,' said a tea master, 'so the
vapour from the tea kettle rises up in the room
where the flowers exhale their scent.'

The guests enter the room noiselessly: only when
all are seated in the correct manner does the host
come in. Those invited sit quietly in silence. The
freshly brewed tea spreads a fragrance that fills the
room and penetrates the soul by way of the senses.
The meaning of the tea ceremony knows no outwardly attainable goal. Its form and the way that
form is put into practice are prescribed by the
master. No visible result is striven for: no lasting
work for now and for eternity is accomplished.[48]

After decades of zealous practice the tea ceremony, in awe-inspiring fashion, attains its maturity
and calls for self-mastery step by step. The souls of
guest and host surrender their personal selves and
become united with each other. In the reality of this
sphere the antinomy between soul and body is
abolished and grows into harmonious unity. Man
himself has now become a soul in the form of art.
The separateness of existence and being no longer
exists, the soul is freed from the body and man feels
himself a solitary being full of meaning and close
to the essence of things.

In the world of the tea ceremony there ensues an

elevation of the psycho-physical existence in which
the spirit attains freedom to deepen and refine itself.
The significance of the tea ceremony lies in the
return to nature, in unification and fusion with it.
The tea-experience is a miniature world-experience
taking place in the tea room. There we reverence the
poverty of man, the harmony of the world and the
incompleteness of nature. In the noise of the boiling
water we hear the living strength of the sea; in the
steam rising from the tea we catch the scent of pines
on a distant hill. The flowers in the corner point to
the beauty of modesty and the joyous reflection of
life. On all occasions calling for reverence we speak
in the language of flowers. Under the slope of the
overhanging roof sunbeams stream down and
soften the atmosphere.

The various artistic objects which are handled in
the course of the ceremony—tea cup, tea caddy, tea
cloth and so on—give training in plastic perception
through the sense of touch. There are flowers in the
middle of the room: above them hangs a painting
which assists absorption into the cosmos of world
symbolism. The architecture of the tea room and the
surrounding garden is a finished work of art, yet it
flows away into the landscape and into the nature
of the cosmos. By way of environment the tea room
creates art and an abode of art, in which, in a pure

still atmosphere, men sit together in harmony and mutual respect.

The principles of the 'Cha-DO'—harmony, respect, purity, and stillness—are the typical Japanese reactions to life in the true sense of the word. They are also in general the elements necessary for human life in society. In the tea ceremony we find the idealized state of the pristine life of mankind. Harmony symbolizes the nobility of the spirit.

The tea room itself must be harmonious in form. Harmony must exist between the simple sense of touch and the light, harmony in sound and form.

Respect is reverence for man and for nature. Man is not to regard himself as worthy of reverence. Accordingly he must, though conscious how narrow humanity is, transcend his own limitations. This transcendence is based on simplicity and modesty—what the Romans called 'sinceritas'.

Purity means utter cleanliness and beauty of soul and body within the total environing atmosphere which alone makes contemplation of the absolute possible.

The fourth principle is stillness. 'Stillness' means not only quiet internally and externally, but also an inwardly echoing intellectual-aesthetic poverty. 'Wabi', the most essential mark of stillness, is that inexpressible, inward, quiet joy which lies deep hidden in poverty and modesty. In 'Wabi' the beautiful is joyously fused with morality and spirit.

Joy is the breath of the community of intercourse between guest and host. Communication between the two requires few words. The tea room is sparsely furnished. Barely nine square yards contain the world of common inner fullness of agreement. The tea room is the room of non-repetition of daily life. No colour, no shape, no pattern may be repeated. Every object is subjected to rigorous selection. Every individual thing has its proper value and *raison d'être*. There is conversation about plastic art and poetry, conducted in forms of expression which, though outwardly sparing, are of the highest distinction. There is no unveiling: no change takes place in secrecy. For no word, no explanation, can touch the essence of art. Stillness is the way to knowledge itself. It creates the supreme state of the eternal present in which all ideals flow together in the Nothing.

The wisdom of ages with its thousand experiences; the unshakeable factual knowledge of modern science and technique; the sounds of music rich in emotion and variation; the glory of works of art—all fade and die before the depth and strength of the Nothing. Not to return from these into the world of the soul, but unswervingly to take upon oneself contradiction as contradiction; to maintain and elevate as a whole the original purity of soul and body; to bring truth and reality into harmony and to experience them so—that is the profound meaning of artistic activity.[49] The aim of art, however, is not the one-sided promotion of spirit, soul, and senses, but the opening of all human capacities—thought, feeling, and will—to the life rhythm of the world of nature: so will the voiceless voice be heard and the self be brought into harmony with it. The body is now a crystal from which the soul shines forth. The wind drives the clouds hither and thither. The wind is mournful and harsh, but life fluctuates, changes, and weaves its web.

To experience eternity in temporality, to experience in a small space that cosmos in which every existing thing is manifested—that is the essence of art. The sun has set. We sit in the tea room in utter quiet and 'on a moonlit evening, over a steaming cup of tea, catch sight between the garden trees of the shadowy far-off hills beside the lake'.[50] We hear the voices of the cosmos. Heaven, earth, and man compose the picture in supreme harmony. The world is full of poetry. Moreover, there arises no doubt of the meaning of existence in life, or of its contradictory reality, its so and not otherwise, its no less and no more. There is now no life and no death. Man is there and not there: he is at rest in the Nothing. In such a suspension of time the experience of art attains 'DO', its highest peak; and man breathes and rests immediately in God.

> The ocean bed of my soul
> Is deep.
> Neither joy
> Nor the wave of sorrow
> Can there arise.
>
> KITARO NISHIDA [51]

POSTSCRIPT

THIS LITTLE book grew only in part out of the author's own research and observation. Its coming into being was made possible by a small circle of persons interested in the treasures of the Japanese spirit. The book represents mainly the content of a number of lectures delivered in Switzerland and Germany. On this occasion the profound thanks of the author are particularly due to Kitaro Nishida, Daisetz Suzuki, Robert Schinzinger, Kenji Moriya, Tsuneyashi Tsuzumi, and Junya Kitayama. This book stands in the fullest sense on the basis of their thought.

In the composition of the work I have had extraordinary help from a number of learned persons. Professor Luyten of Fribourg, Professor Thomas Ohm of Münster, and Professor Maria Feigl of Bonn were good enough to read individual sections of the manuscript and to offer valuable comments, suggestions, and advice.

My friends Hermann Husmann and Friedrich

Postscript

Reckling co-operated actively in the writing of the book. Without their help it would never have appeared in this form. I am also under an obligation to several academic circles in Münster.

In addition I offer my warm thanks to Frau von Mangoldt, whose appreciation helped this book to appear, and to Herr von Fritsch, of the Otto Wilhelm Barth Verlag, who kindly put himself to so much trouble on my behalf. My best thanks go likewise to Dr. Wany of the Bavarian State Library in Munich. The pictures in this book were made available by the kind assistance of that library.

T. HASUMI

Fribourg
June 1959

APPENDIX

THOUGHTS ON JAPANESE ZEN POETRY

AS THE highest achievement of poetic creation in Japan, Haiku poetry occupies a special place. The Japanese soul finds its clearest expression in thus giving form to the poetic experience in seventeen syllables. In it clarity, economical use of words, and mystical experience are perfected in inward unity.

Haiku poetry constitutes a special phenomenon in the world of literature as a whole. Poet and words are indivisible, for the words mediate the soul of the poet. This purely psychic attitude of the Haiku poet despises any exaggerated verbal expression. Words are holy, as the Buddhists say, and they must be pronounced with reverence as the once-for-all, not to be repeated, medium of the soul going forth from itself. Every word has absolute value and meaning. Generally speaking, there is no possibility of altera-

Every individual character is
the entire poem.

The notion of substitution, revision, becomes impossible in this light.
If, as the Nippon Shoki says, every word has been imbued with a unique soul,

tion, no substitute for a word so pregnant with value.

Nippon Shoki, the oldest Japanese history, reports that in ancient times, the Japanese believed in a god who ruled over the kingdom of words, every word being allotted a soul. This god was called 'Koto-Dama'.

Haiku poetry is still alive as a creation of the speech of today. The Haiku poets are not playing word games like the Renga poets: they are priests of speech in the true sense. Their works are an un-mediated expression of their soul's commerce with the Absolute.

Like other artists, the Haiku poets are not con-cerned with the visible expression completing itself step by step in the creative process, but proceed beyond it until the work is completed inwardly. This external incompleteness is part and parcel of the characteristic features of Japanese verbal art.

The peculiarity of Haiku poetry lies in the brevity of the formulation. This, however, is sus-tained by a peculiar motif and content. The experience of which Haiku creation is a result lies in the relation established between man and God. Its striving and creating betoken purely and simply the absorption of the human soul. The farther a man travels on the way to the deep ground, the purer does the original source well up from it.

Whereas the Western spirit applies its mind to the ground of being in logical fashion, the Japanese plunges into the task of sounding the depths of that ground with the totality of the soul, intuitively. In Haiku poetry the deepest ground of Japanese poetry became manifest. Yet the path of Japanese literature required a period of 900 years for the slow attainment of its summit in Haiku. The earliest literary creation developed in periods of realistic naturalism and early romanticism, in which, mediated through pure feeling, it reached poetic expression (Mannyo poetry collection, A.D. 759, Kokin collection, A.D. 905). Pure feeling embraces nature as well as human life in a simultaneous community and recollection of experience. No rigid distinction is drawn between life and nature. They also form a totality plunged into the depths of the human soul. The basic conception of this artistic creation is 'naturalness', one of the categories of Japanese art. Cosmos and soul were, in the sense of the natural, pure subjectivity, and, in the same sense, pure objectivity. The other world and this world exist only in an immanent reality.

Men were living in the world of space and time, and so the temper of their aesthetic was like an expression of the experience of cosmic totality in which the world of space and time is included. This experience of pure subjective-objective reality is the basis of artistic inspiration in the history of every people. In this experience Buddhism was able to reveal itself to the Japanese people.

Religious experience through art passed progressively into a new and genuine form. Perhaps it was a case of a psychic uplifting of what was naturally given.

From this transcendental horizon of the experience of the cosmos, the soul turned inward. Now, in opposition to the transcendence of Buddha-centralism and its penetration, human life constituted the centre. By the path through experience of the cosmos the soul found its way back to itself, but not now in the same form as previously. Immanence enters deeply into the return of the soul to itself. The intention of Japanese romanticism was directed towards nature. But not by the path of an almost tragic experience. The abyss between man and nature was not as wide as that. The Buddhism of the Tendai and Shingon schools, which made its sudden entry into the Japanese life of the soul about the middle of the ninth century, deepened the basic ground of the Japanese soul, and made it possible to unify the inward experience in man and the natural relation with the world and with life.

In his community with nature and his yearning for eternal love the Japanese was in search of that absoluteness that is the principal feature of romanticism: tragedy at the end of man's life is unavoidable. This basic mood in romanticism is characterized by the concept of 'Mono-no-Aware' and implies in this context a pure aesthetic atmosphere radiated by life and things. 'Mono-no-Aware' is the yearning after a basic ground of the eternal.

All joy seeks the eternal. All love yearns for the Absolute. In the same way as the idea of eternity is inherent in life within time, or the feeling for life lies hidden in the essential search for the eternal, tragedy is the yearning for the Absolute. The romantic experience always involves a sad destiny, but it leads to renunciation of the world and penetration into eternity.

Japanese romanticism arose out of the experience of inevitable fate. It gave form to the romantic flowering of the Hei-an period and passed slowly over into the Zen experience of the following period. The romantic spirit of the age was filled with the yearning for absoluteness. Whereas its refinement was nothing but a soft and feminine sentiment, its trend mounted by way of a sensualist experience of the world.

The feminine refinement of romanticism collapsed

before the historical necessity of the new power of knighthood. But its echo disclosed the other aspect of the eternal, the shadow of dreams, the eternal growth in the Nothing.

Harsh experience shaped the Japanese soul; the decorative colour of its romantic world declined, and it entered an historic period. The stern masculine inward law of knighthood went hand in hand with the Zen experience as far as the ultimate abyss and penetrated into an absolute solitude.

> Swept away by the flood
> How abandoned I feel,
> Alone on the high sea.
> No rescuing vessel is in sight.
>
> PRIEST SAIGYO

The path of the Japanese soul led through the poetry of solitude which reconciled Buddhism and romanticism. The former consciousness of clarity, simplicity, and naturalness came to life once more. After concentrating on the world of solitude, Saigyo returned to the old world, but at a deeper level of experience of consciousness of the world. The self, until today the centre of the world, will tomorrow be no more than a dewdrop on a bamboo leaf in the shade. By virtue of this experience the I is swept away in the NOTHING, and there remains only a trace, like the end of a dream.

97

History is only transcended through time
Being mediates No-thingness

Appendix

I am so weary
Of wandering.
Now death comes upon me;
I am alone like the drops
That fall from the leaves.

PRIEST SAIGYO

The Japanese soul sank behind the shadows of the
fading horizon. It did not diffuse itself in an earthly
world, but transcended history through time by
absorption into the immanent world where the
voices of the ground of being can be heard.
Thus:

Through the mists veiling
The dimly seen mountains,
My ear faintly catches
The sad belling of a deer.

PRIEST SAIGYO

In that world all self-experiences were abolished.
It is not the individual man that is eternal; his works
and all that he sets store by last only so long as
history remains alive. The development of a tradition of this kind takes place not only in the specific
field of religious experience: it strikes root in the
profound primal consciousness, in the Zen experience, and seeks stillness and austerity of form from
which the inessential has been eliminated.

I live thus alone
Where no one visits me.
Yet in the depth of the night
The clear light of the moon
Seeks out even my cabin.

HUJIWARA NO TOSHINARI

The essence of this soul-experience was called 'the beauty of secret distance and depth' (Yugen-bi). Behind hiddenness the yet deeper Something was sought. To see revelation in distance, to experience the hidden in the depths—that is within the power only of the man who perceives the Absolute in the multiplicity of the world, and recognizes God in the breath of nature. Distance is transcendence in space, and depth is immanence through time. Transcendence-immanence of this kind no longer appears to be capable of form. It is never more than a hint, by way of expression, at distance and depth.

The evening hour;
An autumn wind from the field
Pierces deep into my heart;
And quails cry
In the thickets of Hukagusa.

HUJIWARA NO TOSHINARI

The poet forsakes the place where the power of the world is supreme: that which cries near at hand, that which ravishes and transports, fall silent in infinity. In him and around him is stillness only.

The absolute objectivization of everything visible and sensible in existence took place once more in the experience of the transcendent and immanent world. The formation of the Japanese psychic experience found a way of penetrating to the frontier of powerful self-mastery. That which is personal and that which is common to humanity makes itself known only in a reflection of the cosmic voice.

Full of power
The waves roll in thunder,
Tearing, dashing,
Breaking
On the rocks of the shore.

MINAMOTO NO SANETOMO

The more powerful the self-mastery, the stronger the reflection of infinity. The self has but one ground of existence, and that is mastered through itself. The 'Self' is violently overcome by means of the transcendent and immanent experience of the world. This process is not carried out in the external world or in objective history, but in the world of the spirit. It was this world of experience that was the source of Haiku poetry, of the world of Basho.

This immanent depth and its world manifest themselves in him as poetic experience, in which the voiceless voices are in concord with those of the eternal in nature.

> The temple bell
> Sounds far and near
> On an evening of summer.
>
> BASHO

Basho's work is called the world of 'Sabi' or 'Yugen'. Sabi is the expression of the eternal experienced, which, on the far side of the common round and of all worldly appearances, encounters all that exists, lives, and dies. Sabi connotes solitude, stillness, repose. For the great artists or philosophers solitude means mastery of creative potentiality in its inmost self. By way of solitude the soul touches the Absolute.

> Whiter than the stone
> On the rocky mountain
> Is the autumn wind.
>
> BASHO

White is the colour of solitude. Basho looks at the whiteness of the rocks and from the depths of his soul ascribes that whiteness to the autumn wind. He carried stillness in his heart and listened to the deeply silent ground of the NOTHING.

Appendix

The whole life of a Japanese who has turned inward, based as it is on the reality of solitude, death, and life, is a challenge, despite the 'way' to be trodden. Man grows beyond death and touches the essence of being which reposes in the NOTHING.

Basho sums up the essence of things in two categories: NOTHING and being. He who plays with the NOTHING suffers from being. When one experiences the NOTHING in being and being in NOTHING, then for both one finds CALM in being. Being is by no means explained through being, nor the NOTHING through the NO-THING. By being, by the appearance of the NOTHING the experience of which lies in being, Basho means the experience which brings the development of being to perfection, though not only in works of art.

Slowly
Spring becomes complete
With moonlight and plums.

BASHO

With Basho, being, the task of uplifting which is allocated to the artist and the philosopher, constitutes also the uplifting impulse of the NOTHING, of the contradiction of reality—of the individual self which gives appearance to personality and to the beyond. When man has plunged fully into the NOTHING, in that very moment he rises above his life of appearances, above the contradictions of the world.

After this experience of the Nothing—which the man of Zen likes to call the experience of 'Satori'—had been consciously undergone as primal reality, Basho followed this way farther. As an artist not concerned only with looking and with the experience of consciousness, he sought above all the creative life that arises out of the NOTHING. He liberated himself from himself as contradiction, emerged in appearance and operated simultaneously in the infinite ocean of the NOTHING.

Behind the world of becoming Basho saw the One, the NOTHING, the Absolute. The Japanese call this spiritual experience the 'way'.

> Sick on the journey
> My dream walks
> Through the withered fields.

BASHO

The 'way' is also known as 'change', which means that the soul lingers on as a mirror in the game of heaven and enjoys the earth. For in heaven the path of clear moonlight appears through the soul, and on the earth the flowers bloom through it. With

Basho the game can be called immersion in the primal ground, yet Basho did not go on to forget being.

> Summer grass
> Is all that remained
> Of old soldiers' dreams

BASHO

As concepts and ideas, NOTHING and being stand in mutual opposition, but being—when it transforms itself into the NOTHING experienced —also gains the power to abolish contradiction and the control of appearances.

Everything is active in face of being in the NOTHING, but nothing is active in face of the NOTHING in being. Sorrow—appearance—pain —joy—according to Basho these are the consequences of being. The NOTHING can become real only through the mediation of the experience of being. As a philosopher he means that being is purely and simply the medium for the experience of the Absolute. Concerning this experience the definition of the NOTHING gives the following explanation—the Absolute emerging from the fate of oppositeness. The man who has been delivered enters alone into infinity and at the same time travels the way of eternal stillness.

No one
Walks this way
At nightfall in autumn.

BASHO

As a poet, Basho strove after the Buddhist deliverance which in his life he attained step by step.
With Basho the striving after creation was entirely
realized. Basho's task and work consisted in the
renewal of the eternally sounding rhythm of the
cosmos. His works tell us both of the perception in
which the deep sound of poetic creation vibrates, and
also of the profundity of the poet's attitude of soul.

No one else in Japan had the capacity to hear the
voices of the voiceless and to express them in such
brevity of form. Basho's work was unique in time,
as it was unique in creativity: in face of the world it
proclaims the great achievement of Japanese artistry.
Saigyo's classic poetry, Sogi's chain poetry, Sesshu's
painting, Rikyu's tea art—all are based on the same
experience. A tradition like this lives as a cosmic law
without authority, as a voice without voice, as a
picture without colour or matter, for it is the giving
of form to the uplifting and simplification of
creation manifesting itself in the human soul. Its
voice is stillness, its form the formless, in which fulfilment flows out into itself and transcends the law
of form.

Appendix

Grave mound, be moved!
My wailing voice
Is the autumn wind.

BASHO

In Basho we encounter without mediation the soul-life of Japan. For him God was everything. There did not, however, ensue any irruption of the other world into the human. The soul of Japan goes on to the ultimate spiritualization of the NOTHING.

The Zen experience, however, knows the method of calling forth being from the NO-THING. The art of Japan requires the uplifting of the soul's ability, and inward deepening of spiritual powers in which the primal forces of the ground of being come to life.

The way of Haiku begins in Zen with the trans-formation of being into the NOTHING by the power of the primal ground.

Basho was a poet and at the same time a Zen mystic, who, as an artist, created and illumined his work from the depths of the primal ground of the NOTHING.

Bright moonlight
Shines the whole night through
Around the pond.

106

NOTES

[1] Since there is in the Far East no philosophy in the European
sense of the word, I would prefer, instead of 'philosophy', to
introduce the term 'metaphilosophy'. In the course of progress along the road of knowledge, four steps can be distinguished. For these I wish to employ the traditional Latin
terms:

(1) Intentio recta:
   Understanding of observations;
   Object of the natural sciences.

(2) Intentio obliqua:
   Understanding of abstraction of objects;
   Object of ontology.

(3) Intentio reflexiva:
   Understanding of transcendental connections;
   Object of philosophical understanding.

(4) Intentio intensiva:
   Becoming conscious of consciousness;
   Object of metaphilosophy.

The object of metaphilosophy corresponds to the intelligible world in the philosophy of Nishida. Nishida distinguishes three degrees of objects of philosophy as follows:

(1) Natural world;

(2) World of consciousness;

(3) Intelligible world.

[2] Tanabe, H.: *Concerning Shobo-Genzo*, p. 2.
[3] In this chapter I am indebted for several references to Professor Schinzinger's introduction to *The Intelligible World*. The three elements of the Japanese world outlook are a generally known fact.
[4] Schinzinger's introduction to *The Intelligible World*, p. 26. This definition rests on the basis of Nishida's philosophy. From the pure standpoint of Nishida, Schinzinger's definition is neither precise nor sufficient.
[5] Ibid., p. 26.
[6] Dogen, founder of the Japanese Sodo-Zen school, author of *Shobo-Genzo*, 96 vols.
[7] Nishida, Kitaro, 1871–1945, a leading Japanese philosopher.
[8] Tanabe, Hajime, pupil of Nishida.
[9] On p. 14 of his introduction to *The Intelligible World* Schinzinger emphasizes that Zen is akin to mysticism. But that is false when Zen meditation is seen from the viewpoint of European mysticism.
[10] Ibid, p. 14.
Nishida's constructed dialectic of the Nothing and Tanabe's absolute dialectic.
[11] Suzuki, D. T.: *The Great Deliverance*, Leipzig, 1939, p. 126.
[12] Schinzinger, p. 17.
[13] Ibid., p. 18.
[14] Ibid., p. 33.
[15] Nishida: *The Intelligible World*, p. 163.
[16] Ibid., p. 132.
[17] Schinzinger, p. 34. Nishida: *Philosophical Treatise IV*, new edition, 1950, p. 240. Nishida: *Fundamental Problems of*

Philosophy, New Series, new edition, Tokyo, 1949, p. 450. Nishida: ibid., pp. 445–8.

[18] Schinzinger, p. 35. Nishida: *Philosophical Treatise II*, new edition, 1950, p. 241.

[19] Ibid., p. 37.

[20] Ibid., p. 39.

[21] Ibid., p. 39.

[22] Ibid., p. 20.

[23] In this chapter I am greatly obliged for much advice regarding historical fact to Professor Moriya's *Japanese Painting*, Wiesbaden, 1953.

[24] Muraoka: *Introduction to Japanese Cultural History*, Tokyo, 1938 (in Japanese).

[25] Ibid., p. 24.

[26] Moriya: *Japanese Painting*, Wiesbaden, 1953, p. 46.

[27] Sokan (1464–1552), the most important Renga poet.

[28] Moiya, p. 104.

[29] It is worth noting that in this period scientific philology came into being in Japan and in Germany almost simultaneously.

[30] Moriya, pp. 126–7.

[31] I am indebted for several references in this chapter to Professor Tsuzumi's *The Art of Japan*, Leipzig, 1929. In this work he also touches on the categories of Japanese art. But the concept of 'complementarity' cannot be found among his categories, though this is the most important attribute of the categories of Japanese art.

These categories are a generally recognized concept in Japan.

[32] Tsuzumi: *The Art of Japan*, Leipzig, 1929, p. 17.

[33] See p. 20 above, and ibid., p. 21.

[34] See p. 23 above.

[35] Tsuzumi, p. 22.

[36] Ibid., p. 23.

[37] I am obliged for some valuable references in this chapter to Professor Moriya's *Japanese Painting*.

[38] See p. 19 above.

[39] See p. 20 above, and Moriya, p. 20.

[40] See Chapter III above, and Moriya, p. 20.

[41] See Moriya, pp. 29–31.

[42] Ibid., p. 31.

[43] In this chapter I am deeply indebted for advice and valuable references to Professor Kitayama's *East-West Encounter*, Berlin, 4th edition, 1954. The concept 'DO' really arose from Confucianism. But the Japanese were the first to embrace 'DO' as the art of living.

[44] Kitayama, p. 122.

[45] These steps in the experience of truth originate from the Zen teaching 'Ten Oxen Pictures'.

[46] See H. Hammitzsch: *Cha-do, the Tea Way*, O. W. Barth-Verlag, 1958.

[47] Kitayama, p. 123.

[48] Ibid., p. 123.

[49] Ibid., pp. 124–6. Nishida: *Fundamental Problems of Philosophy*, new edition, Tokyo, 1949, pp. 446–50.

[50] This expression has been used by the tea masters for centuries.

[51] Schinzinger, p. 25.

BIBLIOGRAPHY

Von Dürckheim, Karlfried, The Japanese Cult of Tranquillity, (translated by Eda O'Shiel), Rider, London, 1960.

Dogen, Shobo-Genzo (in Japanese).

Hammitzsch, Horst, Cha-Do, the Tea Way (in German), O. W. Barth-Verlag, Munich, 1958.

Herrigel, Eugen, Zen in the Art of Archery (English translation by R. F. C. Hull), Routledge and Kegan Paul, London, 1953.

— The Method of Zen (translated by R. F. C. Hull) Routledge and Kegan Paul, London, 1957.

Herrigel, Gusti L., Zen in the Art of Flower Arrangement, Routledge and Kegan Paul, London, 1956.

Hujimura, Tsukuru, Kokobungakushi Sosetsu (Introduction to Japanese Philology), Tokyo, 1951.

Kitayama, Junya, East-West Encounter (in German), Berlin, 4th edition, 1954.

Moriya, Kenji, Japanese Painting (in German), Wiesbaden, 1953.

Muraoka, Tsunetsugu, Introduction to Japanese Cultural History (in Japanese), Tokyo, 1954.

Nishida, Kitaro, The Intelligible World, Three Philosophical Essays (in German), Berlin, 1943.

— Nishida's writings (all in Japanese)
   1. Concerning the Good.

Bibliography

2. Thought and Experience.
3. Perception and Reflection in Self-consciousness.
4. The Problem of Self-consciousness.
5. Art and Morals.
6. From the Working to the Seeing.
7. The Self-consciousness of the Universal.
8. The Self-determination of the Nothing.
9. Fundamental Problems of Philosophy—The World of Activity.
10. Fundamental Problems of Philosophy, New Series—The Dialectical World.
11. Collection of Philosophical Papers, I.
12. Collection of Philosophical Papers, II.
13. Collection of Philosophical Papers, III.
14. Collection of Philosophical Papers, IV.
15. Collection of Philosophical Papers, V.
16. Collection of Philosophical Papers, VI.
17. Thought and Experience, New Series.

Nishida, Naojiro, Survey of Japanese Cultural History (in Japanese), Kyoto, 1932.

Okakura, Kakuzo, The Book of Tea (in German), Inselverlag, 1949.

— The Ideals of the East with Special Reference to the Art of Japan, 1903.

Origuchi, Shinobu, Introduction to Japanese Literature (in Japanese), Tokyo, 1957.

Lüth, Paul, Japanese Philosophy. Quest for a Complete Representation having regard to the Beginnings in Myth and Religion (in German), Tübingen, 1944.

Seami, Ka–den–sho (in Japanese), 1401.

Suzuki, D. T., Living by Zen, O. W. Barth-Verlag, Munich, 1955.

The Philosophy of art
in Japanese Zen

Bibliography

— Zen and Japanese Culture, London, 1959.

— The Great Deliverance, Zürich, 1958.

Tanabe, Hajime, Examination of Mathematical Philosophy (in Japanese), Tokyo, 1925.

— Introduction to Philosophy (in Japanese), Tokyo, 1933.

— Concerning Shobo-Genzo (in Japanese), Tokyo.

Tsuji, Zennosuke, Japanese Culture and Buddhism (in Japanese), new edition, Tokyo, 1951.

Tsuzumi, Tsuneyoshi, The Art of Japan (in German), Leipzig, 1929.

Lightning Source UK Ltd.
Milton Keynes UK
UKHW022019210222
399032UK00003B/399

I will kill myself.
Soon. But when I see your face,
I think: not today.

On a   muddy bank
a gray fish writhes
praying hard for death.